A GUIDE TO CLAIMS-BASED IDENTITY AND ACCESS CONTROL

A GUIDE TO
Claims-Based Identity and Access Control

Authentication and Authorization for Services and the Web

patterns & practices
Microsoft Corporation

ISBN: 9780735640597

Contents

Foreword

Claims-based identity means to control the digital experience and to use digital resources based on things that are said by one party about another. A party can be a person, organization, government, Web site, Web service, or even a device. The very simplest example of a claim is something that a party says about itself.

As the authors of this book point out, there is nothing new about the use of claims. As far back as the early days of mainframe computing, the operating system asked users for passwords and then passed each new application a "claim" about who was using it. But this world was a kind of "Garden of Eden" because applications didn't question what they were told.

As systems became interconnected and more complicated, we needed ways to identify parties across multiple computers. One way to do this was for the parties that used applications on one computer to authenticate to the applications (and/or operating systems) that ran on the other computers. This mechanism is still widely used—for example, when logging on to a great number of Web sites.

However, this approach becomes unmanageable when you have many co-operating systems (as is the case, for example in the enterprise). Therefore, specialized services were invented that would register and authenticate users, and subsequently provide claims about them to interested applications. Some well-known examples are NTLM, Kerberos, Public Key Infrastructure (PKI), and the Security Assertion Markup Language (SAML).

If systems that use claims have been around for so long, how can "claims-based computing" be new or important? The answer is a variant of the old adage that "All tables have legs, but not all legs have tables." The claims-based model embraces and subsumes the capabilities of all the systems that have existed to date, but it also allows many new things to be accomplished. This book gives a great sense of the resultant opportunities.

For one thing, identity no longer depends on the use of unique identifiers. NTLM, Kerberos, and public key certificates conveyed, above all else, an identification number or name. This unique number could be used as a directory key to look up other attributes and to track activities. But once we start thinking in terms of claims-based computing, identifiers were not mandatory. We don't need to say that a person is associated with the number X, and then look in a database to see if number X is married. We just say the person is married. An identifier is reduced to one potential claim (a thing said by some party) among many.

This opens up the possibility of many more directly usable and substantive claims, such as a family name, a person's citizenship, the right to do something, or the fact that someone is in a certain age group or is a great customer. One can make this kind of claim without revealing a party's unique identity. This has immense implications for privacy, which becomes an increasingly important concern as digital identity is applied to our personal lives.

Further, while the earlier systems were all hermetic worlds, we can now look at them as examples of the same thing and transform a claim made in one world to a claim made in another. We can use "claims transformers" to convert claims from one system to another, to interpret meanings, apply policies, and to provide elasticity. This is what makes claims essential for connecting our organizations and enterprises into a cloud. Because they are standardized, we can use them across platforms and look at the distributed fabric as a real circuit board on which we can assemble our services and components.

Claims offer a single conceptual model, programming interface, and end-user paradigm; whereas before claims, we had a cacophony of disjoint approaches. In my experience, the people who use these new approaches to build products universally agree that they solve many pressing problems that were impossibly difficult before. Yet these people also offer a word of advice. Though embracing what has existed, the claims-based paradigm is fundamentally a new one; the biggest challenge is to understand this and take advantage of it.

That's why this book is so useful. It deals with the fundamental issues, but it is practical and concise. The time spent reading it will be repaid many times over as you become an expert in one of the transformative technologies of our time.

Kim Cameron
Distinguished Engineer—Microsoft Identity Division

Foreword

In the spring of 2008, months before the Windows Identity Foundation made its first public appearance, I was on the phone with the chief software architect of a Fortune 500 company when I experienced one of those vivid, clarifying moments that come during the course of a software project. We were chatting about how difficult it was to manage an environment with hundreds or even thousands of developers, all building different kinds of applications for different audiences. In such an environment, the burden of consistent application security usually falls on the shoulders of one designated security architect.

A big part of that architect's job is to guide developers on how to handle authentication. Developers have many technologies to choose from. Windows Integrated Authentication, SAML, LDAP, and X.509 are just a few. The security architect is responsible for writing detailed implementation guidance on when and how to use all of them. I imagined a document with hundreds of pages of technology overviews, decision flowcharts, and code appendices that demonstrate the correct use of technology *X* for scenario *Y*. "If you are building a Web application, for employees, on the intranet, on Windows, use Windows Integrated Authentication and LDAP, send your queries to the enterprise directory...."

I could already tell that this document, despite the architect's best efforts, was destined to sit unread on the corner of every developer's desk. It was all just too hard; although every developer knows security is important, no one has the time to read all that. Nevertheless, *every* organization needed an architect to write these guidelines. It was the only meaningful thing they could do to manage this complexity.

It was at that moment that I realized the true purpose of the forthcoming Windows Identity Foundation. It was to render the technology decision trivial. *Architects would no longer need to create complex guidelines for authentication.* This was an epiphany of sorts.

Windows Identity Foundation would allow authentication logic to be factored out of the application logic, and as a result most developers would never have to deal with the underlying complexity. Factoring out authentication logic would insulate applications from changing requirements. Making an application available to users at multiple organizations or even moving it to the cloud would just mean reconfiguring the identity infrastructure and not rewriting the application code. This refactoring of identity logic is called the claims-based identity model.

Eugenio Pace from the Microsoft patterns & practices group has brought together some of the foremost minds on this topic so that their collective experience can be yours. He has focused on practical scenarios that will help you get started writing your own claims-aware applications. The guide works progressively, with the simplest and most common scenarios explained first. It also contains a clear overview of the main concepts. Working source code for all of the examples can be found online (http://claimsid.codeplex.com).

I have truly enjoyed having Eugenio be part of our extended engineering team during this project. His enthusiasm, creativity, and perseverance have made this book possible. Eugenio is one of the handful of people I have met who revel in the challenge of identity and security and who care deeply that it be done right.

Our goal is for this book to earn its way to the corner of your desk and lie there dog-eared and much referenced, so that we can be your identity experts and you can get on with the job that is most important to you, building applications that matter. We wish you much success.

Stuart Kwan
Group Program Manager, Identity and Access Platform
Microsoft Corporation
Redmond, Washington
January 2010

Preface

As an application designer or developer, imagine a world where you don't have to worry about authentication. Imagine instead that all requests to your application already include the information you need to make access control decisions and to personalize the application for the user.

In this world, your applications can trust another system component to securely provide user information, such as the user's name or e-mail address, a manager's e-mail address, or even a purchasing authorization limit. The user's information always arrives in the same simple format, regardless of the authentication mechanism, whether it's Microsoft® Windows® integrated authentication, forms-based authentication in a Web browser, an X.509 client certificate, or something more exotic. Even if someone in charge of your company's security policy changes how users authenticate, you still get the information, and it's always in the same format.

This is the utopia of claims-based identity that *A Guide to Claims-Based Identity and Access Control* describes. As you'll see, claims provide an innovative approach for building applications that authenticate and authorize users.

Who This Book Is For

This book gives you enough information to evaluate claims-based identity as a possible option when you're planning a new application or making changes to an existing one. It is intended for any architect, developer, or information technology (IT) professional who designs, builds, or operates Web applications and services that require identity information about their users. Although applications that use claims-based identity exist on many platforms, this book is written for people who work with Windows-based systems. You should be familiar with the Microsoft .NET Framework, ASP.NET, Windows Communication Foundation (WCF), and Microsoft Visual C#®.

Why This Book Is Pertinent Now

Although claims-based identity has been possible for quite a while, there are now tools available that make it much easier for developers of Windows-based applications to implement it. These tools include the Windows Identity Foundation (WIF) and Microsoft Active Directory® Federation Services (ADFS) v2. This book shows you when and how to use these tools in the context of some commonly occurring scenarios.

A Note About Terminology

This book explains claims-based identity without using a lot of new terminology. However, if you read the various standards and much of the existing literature, you'll see terms such as "relying party," "STS," "subject," "identity provider," and so on. Here is a short list that equates some of the most common expressions used in the literature with the more familiar terms used in this book. For additional clarification about terminology, see the glossary at the end of the book.

RELYING PARTY (RP) = APPLICATION
SERVICE PROVIDER (SP) = APPLICATION

A relying party or a service provider is an application that uses claims. The term "relying party" arose because the application relies on an issuer to provide information about identity. The term "service provider" is commonly used with the Security Assertion Markup Language (SAML). Because this book is intended for people who design and build applications, it uses "application," or "claims-aware application," instead of "relying party," "RP," "service provider" or "SP."

SUBJECT = USER
PRINCIPAL = USER

A subject or a principal is a user. The term "subject" has been around for years in security literature, and it does make sense when you think about it—the user is the subject of access control, personalization, and so on. A subject can be a non-human entity, such as printer or another device, but this book doesn't discuss these scenarios. In addition, the .NET Framework uses the term "principal" rather than "subject." This book talks about "users" rather than "subjects" or "principals."

SECURITY TOKEN SERVICE (STS) = ISSUER

Technically, a security token service is the interface within an issuer that accepts requests and creates and issues security tokens containing claims.

IDENTITY PROVIDER (IDP) = ISSUER

An identity provider is an issuer or a "token issuer," if you prefer. Identity providers validate various user credentials, such as user names and passwords, and certificates, and they issue tokens. For brevity, this book uses the term "issuer."

RESOURCE SECURITY TOKEN SERVICE (R-STS) = ISSUER

A resource security token service accepts one token and issues another. Rather than having information about identity, it has information about the resource. For example, an R-STS can translate tokens issued by an identity provider into application-specific claims.

For this book, there's no point in separating the functions of an identity provider, a security token service, and a resource security token service. In fact, much of the existing literature lazily mixes these up, anyway, which just adds to the confusion. This book uses the more practical term, "issuer," to encompass all these concepts.

ACTIVE CLIENT = SMART OR RICH CLIENT
PASSIVE CLIENT = BROWSER

Much of the literature refers to "active" versus "passive" clients. An active client can use a sophisticated library such as Windows Communication Foundation (WCF) to implement the protocols that request and pass around security tokens (WS-Trust is the protocol used in active scenarios). In order to support many different browsers, the passive scenarios use a much simpler protocol to request and pass around tokens that rely on simple HTTP primitives such as HTTP GET (with redirects) and POST. (This simpler protocol is defined in the WS-Federation specification, section 13.)

In this book, an active client is a rich client or a smart client. A passive client is a Web browser.

How This Book Is Structured

You can think of the structure of this book as a subway that has main stops and branches. After the preface, there are two chapters that contain general information. These are followed by scenarios that show how to apply this knowledge with increasingly more sophisticated requirements.

Here is the map of our subway.

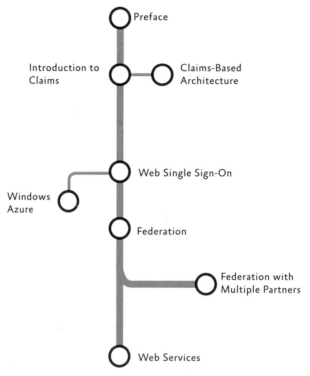

FIGURE 1
Map of the book

"An Introduction to Claims" explains what a claim is and gives general rules on what makes a good claim and how to incorporate them in your application. It's probably a good idea that you read this chapter before you go on to the scenarios.

"Claims-Based Architectures" shows you how to use claims with browser-based applications and smart client–based applications. In particular, the chapter focuses on how to implement single sign-on for your users, whether they are on an intranet or an extranet. This chapter is optional. You don't need to read it before you go on to the scenarios.

"Claims-Based Single Sign-On for the Web" shows you how to implement single-sign on within a corporate intranet. Although this may be something that you can also implement with Windows integrated authentication, it is the first stop on the way to implementing more complex scenarios. It includes a section for Windows Azure™ that shows you how to move the claims-based application to the cloud.

"Federated Identity for Web Applications" shows you how you can give your business partners access to your applications while maintaining the integrity of your corporate directory and theirs. In other words, your partners' employees can use their corporate credentials to gain access to your applications.

"Federated Identity for Web Services" shows you how to use the claims-based approach with Web services, where a partner uses a smart client rather than a browser.

"Federated Identity with Multiple Partners" is a variation of the previous scenario that shows you how to federate with partners who have no issuer of their own as well as those who do. It demonstrates how to use the ASP.NET MVC framework to create a claims-aware application.

What You Need to Use the Code

You can either run the scenarios on your own system or you can create a realistic lab environment. Running the scenarios on your own system is very simple and has only a few requirements. These are the system requirements for running the scenarios on your system:

- Microsoft Windows Vista SP1, Windows 7, or Microsoft Windows Server 2008 (32-bit or 64-bit)
- Microsoft Internet Information Services (IIS) 7.0
- Microsoft .NET Framework 3.5 SP1
- Microsoft Visual Studio® 2008 SP1
- Windows Azure Tools for Microsoft Visual Studio
- Windows Identity Foundation

Running the scenarios in a realistic lab environment, with an instance of Active Directory Federation Services (ADFS) and Active Directory, requires an application server, ADFS, Active Directory, and a client system. Here are their system requirements.

APPLICATION SERVER

The application server requires the following:

- Windows Server 2008
- Microsoft IIS 7.0
- Microsoft Visual Studio 2008 SP1
- .NET Framework 3.5 SP1
- Windows Identity Foundation

ADFS

The ADFS server requires the following:

- Windows Server 2008
- Internet Information Services (IIS) 7.0
- .NET Framework 3.5 SP1
- SQL Server® 2005/2008 Express Edition

ACTIVE DIRECTORY

The Active Directory system requires a Windows server 2008 with Active Directory installed.

CLIENT COMPUTER

The client computer requires Windows Vista or Windows 7 for active scenarios. Passive scenarios may use any Web browser as the client that supports redirects

Who's Who

As we've said, this book uses a set of scenarios that traces the evolution of several corporate applications. A panel of experts comments on the development efforts. The panel includes a security specialist, a software architect, a software developer, and an IT professional. The scenarios can be considered from each of these points of view. Here are our experts.

Bharath is a security specialist. He checks that solutions for authentication and authorization reliably safeguard a company's data. He is a cautious person, for good reasons.

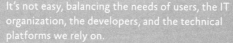

Providing authentication for a single application is easy. Securing all applications across our organization is a different thing.

Jana is a software architect. She plans the overall structure of an application. Her perspective is both practical and strategic. In other words, she considers not only what technical approaches are needed today, but also what direction a company needs to consider for the future.

It's not easy, balancing the needs of users, the IT organization, the developers, and the technical platforms we rely on.

Markus is a senior software developer. He is analytical, detail-oriented, and methodical. He's focused on the task at hand, which is building a great claims-based application. He knows that he's the person who's ultimately responsible for the code.

I don't care what you use for authentication, I'll make it work.

Poe is an IT professional who's an expert in deploying and running in a corporate data center. He's also an Active Directory guru. Poe has a keen interest in practical solutions; after all, he's the one who gets paged at 3:00 AM when there's a problem.

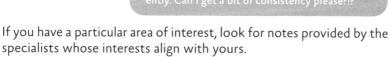

Each application handles authentication differently. Can I get a bit of consistency please?!?

If you have a particular area of interest, look for notes provided by the specialists whose interests align with yours.

Acknowledgments

This book marks a milestone in a journey I started in the winter of 2007. At that time, I was offered the opportunity to enter a completely new domain, the world of software delivered as a service. Offerings such as Windows Azure were far from being realized, and "the cloud" was still to be defined and fully understood. My work mainly focused on uncovering the specific challenges that companies would face with this new way of delivering software.

It was immediately obvious that managing identity and access control was a major obstacle for developers. Identity and access control were fundamental. They were prerequisites for everything else. If you didn't get authentication and authorization right, you would be building your application on a foundation of sand.

Thus began my journey in the world of claims-based identity. I was very lucky to initiate this journey with none other than a *claims Jedi,* Vittorio Bertocci. He turned me into a convert.

Initially, I was puzzled that so few people were deploying what seemed, at first glance, to be simple principles. Then I understood why. In my discussions with colleagues and customers, I frequently found myself having to think twice about many of the concepts and about the mechanics needed to put them into practice. In fact, even after longer exposure to the subject, I found myself having to carefully retrace the interactions among implementation components. The principles may have been simple, but translating them into running code was a different matter. Translating them into the *right* running code was even harder.

Around this same time, Microsoft announced Windows Identity Foundation, ADFS v2, and Access Control Service. Once I understood how to apply those technologies, and how they dramatically simplified claims-based development, I realized that the moment had come to create a guide like the one you are now reading.

Even after I had spent a significant amount of time on the subject, I realized that providing prescriptive guidance required greater proficiency than my own, and I was lucky to be able to recruit for my quest some very bright and experienced experts. I have thoroughly enjoyed working with them on this project and would be honored to work with this fine team again. I was also fortunate to have skilled software developers, software testers, technical writers, and others as project contributors.

I want to start by thanking the following subject matter experts and key contributors to this guide: Dominick Baier, Vittorio Bertocci, Keith Brown, and Matias Woloski. These guys were outstanding. I admired their rigor, their drive for excellence, and also their commitment to pragmatic solutions.

Running code is a very powerful device for explaining how technology works. Designing sample applications that are both technically and pedagogically sound is no simple task. I want to thank the project's development and test teams for providing that balance: Federico Boerr, Carlos Farre, Diego Marcet, Anant Manuj Mittal, Erwin van der Valk, and Matias Woloski.

This guide is meant to be authoritative and prescriptive in the topics it covers. However, we also wanted it to be simple to understand, approachable, and entertaining, a guide you would find *interesting* and you would *enjoy* reading. We invested in two areas to achieve this: an approachable writing style and an appealing visual design.

A team of technical writers and editors were responsible for the text. They performed the miracle of translating and organizing our jargon- and acronym-plagued drafts, notes, and conversations into clear, readable text. I want to direct many thanks to RoAnn Corbisier, Colin Campbell, Roberta Leibovitz, and Tina Burden for doing such a fine job on that.

The innovative visual design concept used for this guide was developed by Roberta Leibovitz and Colin Campbell (Modeled Computation LLC) who worked with a team of talented designers and illustrators. The book design was created by John Hubbard (eson). The cartoon faces and chapter divisions were drawn by the award-winning Seattle-based cartoonist Ellen Forney. The technical illustrations were adapted from my Tablet PC mock ups by Veronica Ruiz. I want to thank the creative team for giving this guide such a great look.

I also want to thank all the customers, partners, and community members who have patiently reviewed our early content and drafts. You have truly helped us shape this guide. Among those, I want to highlight the exceptional contributions of Zulfiqar Ahmed, Michele Leroux Bustamante (IDesign), Pablo Mariano Cibraro (Tellago Inc), Hernan DeLahitte (DigitFactory), Pedro Felix, Tim Fischer (Microsoft Germany), Mario Fontana, David Hill, Doug Hiller, Jason Hogg, Ezequiel Jadib, Brad Jonas, Seshadri Mani, Marcelo Mas, Vijayavani Nori,

Krish Shenoy, Travis Spencer (www.travisspencer.com), Mario Szpuszta (Sr. Architect Advisor, Microsoft Austria), Chris Tavares, Peter M. Thompson, and Todd West.

Finally, I want to thank Stuart Kwan and Conrad Bayer from the Identity Division at Microsoft for their support throughout. Even though their teams were extremely busy shipping WIF and ADFS, they always found time help us.

Eugenio Pace
Senior Program Manager—patterns & practices
Microsoft Corporation
Redmond, January 2010

1   An Introduction to Claims

This chapter talks about some concepts, such as *claims* and *federated identity,* that may sound new to you. However, many of these ideas have been around for a long time. The mechanics involved in a claims-based approach have a similar flavor to Kerberos, which is one of the most broadly accepted authentication protocols in use today and is also the protocol used by Microsoft® Active Directory® directory service. Federation protocols such as WS-Federation and the Security Assertion Markup Language (SAML) have been with us for many years as interoperable protocols that are implemented on all major technology platforms.

What Do Claims Provide?

To see the power of claims, you might need to change your view of authentication. It's easy to let a particular authentication mechanism constrain your thinking. If you use Windows Integrated authentication (Kerberos or NTLM), you probably think of identity in terms of Windows user accounts and groups. If you use the ASP.NET membership and roles provider, you probably think in terms of user names, passwords, and roles. If you try to determine what the different authentication mechanisms have in common, you can abstract the individual elements of identity and access control into two parts: a single, general notion of claims along with the concept of an issuer or an authority. Thinking in terms of claims and issuers is a powerful abstraction that supports new ways of securing your applications. Because claims involve an explicit trust relationship with an issuer, your application believes a claim about the current user only if it trusts the entity that issued the claim. Trust is explicit in the claims-based approach, not implicit as in other authentication and authorization approaches you may be familiar with.

1

The following table shows the relationships between security tokens, claims, and issuers.

Security token	Claims	Issuer
Windows token. This token is represented as a security identifier (SID). This is a unique value of variable length that is used to identify a security principal or security group in Windows operating systems.	User name and groups.	Domain.
User name token.	User name.	Application.
Certificate.	Examples can include a thumbprint, a subject, or a distinguished name.	Issuer chains to the root.

> You can use claims to implement Role-Based Access Control (RBAC). Roles are claims, but claims can contain more information than roles. Also, you can send claims inside a signed (and possibly encrypted) security token and be certain that they come from a trusted issuer.

❖ *Claims provide a powerful abstraction for identity.*

The claims-based approach to identity makes it easy for users to sign in using Kerberos where it makes sense, but at the same time, it's just as easy for them to use one or more (perhaps more Internet-friendly) authentication techniques, without you having to recode, recompile, or even reconfigure your applications. You can support any authentication technique, some of the most popular being Kerberos, forms authentication, X.509 certificates, smart cards, as well as information cards and others.

NOT EVERY SYSTEM NEEDS CLAIMS

This is an important disclaimer. Companies with a host of internal applications can use Windows Integrated authentication to achieve many of the benefits provided by claims. Active Directory does a great job of storing user identities, and because Kerberos is a part of Windows, your applications don't have to include much authentication logic. As long as every application you build can use Windows integrated authentication, you may have already reached your identity utopia.

However, there are many reasons why you might need something other than Windows authentication. You might have Web-facing applications that are used by people who don't have accounts in your Windows domain. Another reason is that your company has merged with another company and you're having trouble authenticating across two Windows forests that don't (and may never) have a trust relationship. Perhaps you want to share identities with another company that has non-.NET Framework applications or you need to share identities between applications running on different platforms (for example, the Macintosh). These are just a few situations where claims-based identity can be the right choice for you.

CLAIMS SIMPLIFY AUTHENTICATION LOGIC

Most applications include a certain amount of logic that supports identity-related features. Applications that can't rely on Windows Integrated authentication tend to have more of this than applications that do. For example, Web-facing applications that store user names and passwords must handle password reset, lockout, and other issues. Enterprise-facing applications that use Windows Integrated authentication can rely on the domain controller.

But even with Windows Integrated authentication, there are still challenges. Kerberos tickets only give you a user's account and a list of groups. What if your application needs to send e-mail to the user? What if you need the e-mail address of the user's manager? This starts to get complicated quickly, even within a single domain. To go beyond Kerberos's limitations, you need to program Active Directory. This is not a simple task, especially if you want to build efficient Lightweight Directory Access Protocol (LDAP) queries that don't slow down your directory server.

Claims-based identity allows you to factor out the authentication logic from individual applications. Instead of the application determining who the user is, it receives claims that identify the user.

◈ *Claims help you to factor authentication logic out of your applications.*

A FAMILIAR EXAMPLE

Claims-based identity is all around us. A very familiar analogy is the authentication protocol you follow each time you visit an airport. You can't simply walk up to the gate and present your passport or driver's license. Instead, you must first check in at the ticket counter. Here, you present whatever credential makes sense. If you're going overseas, you show your passport. For domestic flights, you present your driver's license. If your children fly with you, they don't need to show anything at all, but the ticket agent asks you their names to provide some level of authentication. After verifying that your picture ID matches your face, the agent looks up your flight and verifies that you've paid for a ticket. Assuming all is in order, you receive a boarding pass that you take to the gate.

A boarding pass is very informative. Gate agents know your name and frequent flyer number (authentication and personalization), your flight number and seating priority (authorization), and perhaps even more. The gate agents have everything that they need to do their jobs efficiently.

There is also special information on the boarding pass. It is encoded in the bar code and/or the magnetic strip on the back. This information (such as a boarding serial number) proves that the pass was issued by the airline and is not a forgery.

In essence, a boarding pass is a signed set of claims made by the airline about you. It states that you are allowed to board a particular flight at a particular time and sit in a particular seat. Of course, agents don't need to think very deeply about this. They simply validate your boarding pass, read the claims on it, and let you board the plane.

It's also important to note that there may be more than one way of obtaining the signed set of claims that is your boarding pass. You might go to the ticket counter at the airport, or you might use the airline's Web site and print your boarding pass at home. The gate agents boarding the flight don't care how the boarding pass was created. They only care that it is an authentic set of claims that give you permission to get on the plane.

In software, this bundle of claims is called a *security token*. Each security token is signed by the *issuer* who created it. A *claims-based application* considers users to be authenticated if they present a valid, signed security token from a trusted issuer. Figure 1 shows the basic pattern for using claims.

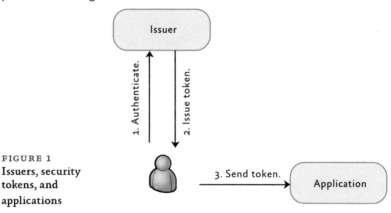

FIGURE 1
Issuers, security tokens, and applications

For an application developer, the advantage of this system is clear: your application doesn't need to worry about what sort of credential the user presents. Someone who determines your company's security policy can make those rules and buy or build the issuer. Your application simply receives the equivalent of a boarding pass. No matter what authentication protocol was used, Kerberos, SSL, forms authentication, or something more exotic, the application gets a signed set of claims that has information it needs about the user. This information is in a simple format that the application can use right away.

WHAT MAKES A GOOD CLAIM?

Security tokens can contain claims such as the user's name, e-mail address, manager's e-mail address, groups, roles, and so on. Think about claims the same way you think about attributes in Active Directory or some other central repository over which you have little control. Depending on your organization, it may be easy or difficult to centralize lots of information about users and issue claims to share that information with applications.

It rarely makes sense to centralize data that is specific to one application only. In fact, even applications that use claims can still benefit from storing a table that contains user information. This table is where you can keep application-specific user data that no other application cares about. This is data for which your application is *authoritative*. In other words, it is the single source for that data, and someone must be responsible for keeping it up to date.

Another use for a table like this is to cache non-authoritative data that you get from claims. For example, you might cache an e-mail claim for each user so that you can send out notification e-mail without the user having to be logged in. You should treat any cached claims as read-only and refresh them the next time the user visits your application and presents fresh claims. Include a date column that you update each time you freshen the record. That way, you know how stale the cached claims have become when it comes time to use them.

When you decide what kinds of claims to issue, ask yourself how hard is it to convince the IT department to extend the Active Directory schema. They have good reasons for staying with what they already have. If they're reluctant now, claims aren't going to change that. Keep this in mind when you choose which attributes to use as claims.

Claims are like salt. Just a little bit flavors the broth. The next chapter has more information on what makes a good claim.

You can also receive tokens that were generated outside of your own realm. This is known as federated identity.

UNDERSTANDING ISSUERS AND ADFS

Today, it's possible to purchase an issuer that provides user information, packaged as claims.

If you have Windows Server 2008 R2 Enterprise Edition, you are automatically licensed to run Microsoft's issuer, Active Directory Federation Services (ADFS) 2.0. ADFS provides the logic to authenticate users in several ways, and you can customize each instance of your ADFS issuer to authenticate users with Kerberos, forms authentication, or certificates. Alternatively, you can ask your ADFS issuer to accept a security token from an issuer in another realm as proof of authentication. This is known as *identity federation* and it's how you achieve single sign-on across realms.

Figure 2 shows all the tasks that the issuer performs.

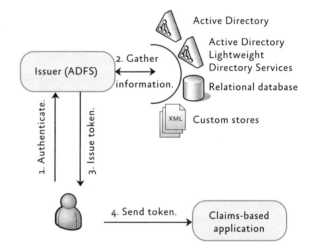

FIGURE 2
ADFS functions

After the user is authenticated, the issuer creates claims about that user and issues a security token. ADFS has a rule engine that makes it easy to extract LDAP attributes from the user's record in Active Directory and its cousin, Lightweight Directory Services. ADFS also allows you to add rules that include arbitrary SQL statements so that you can extract user data out of your own custom SQL database.

You can extend ADFS to add other stores. This is useful because, in many companies, a user's identity is often fragmented. ADFS hides this fragmentation. Your claims-based applications won't break if you decide to move data around between stores. Claims-based applications expect to receive claims about the user, but they don't care about which identity store those claims come from. These applications are loosely coupled to identity. This is one of the biggest benefits of claims-based identity.

Claims-based applications are loosely coupled to identity.

USER ANONYMITY

One option that claims-based applications give you is user anonymity. Remember that your application no longer directly authenticates the users; instead, it relies on an issuer to do that and to make claims about them. If user anonymity is a feature you want, simply don't ask for any claim that personally identifies the user. For example, maybe all you really need is a set of roles to authorize the user's actions, but you don't need to know the user's name. You can do that with claims-based identity by only asking for role claims. Some issuers (such as ADFS) support the idea of private user identifiers, which allows you to get a unique, anonymous identifier for a user without any personal information (such as a name or e-mail address). Keep user anonymity in mind when you consider the power of claims-based identity.

For this to be possible, the issuer must not collude with the application.

Implementing Claims-Based Identity

There are some general set-up steps that every claims-based system requires. Understanding these steps will help you when you read about the claims-based architectures.

STEP 1: ADD LOGIC TO YOUR APPLICATIONS TO SUPPORT CLAIMS

When you build a claims-based application, it needs to know how to validate the incoming security token and how to parse the claims that are inside. The Windows Identity Foundation (WIF) provides a common programming model for claims that can be used by both Windows Communication Foundation (WCF) and ASP.NET applications. If you already know how to use methods such as **IsInRole** and properties such as **Identity.Name**, you'll be happy to know that WIF simply adds one more property that is named **Identity.Claims**. It identifies the claims that were issued, who issued them, and what they contain.

There's certainly more to learn more about WIF programming model, but for now just remember to reference the WIF assembly (**Microsoft.IdentityModel.dll**) from your ASP.NET applications and WCF services in order to use WIF's programming paradigm.

STEP 2: ACQUIRE OR BUILD AN ISSUER

For most teams, the easiest and most secure option will be to use ADFS 2 .0 as the issuer of tokens. Unless you have a great deal of security experience on your team, you should look to the experts to supply an issuer. That's why ADFS 2.0 is a good option for most people. If you need to customize the issuer and the extensibility points in ADFS 2.0 aren't sufficient, you can license third-party software or use WIF to build your own issuer. Note, however, that implementing a production-grade issuer requires specialized skills that are beyond the scope of this book.

STEP 3: CONFIGURE YOUR APPLICATION TO TRUST THE ISSUER

After you build a claims-based application and have an issuer to support it, the next step is to set up a trust relationship. An application trusts its issuer to identify and authenticate users and make claims about their identities. When you configure an application to rely on a specific issuer, you are establishing a *trust* (or *trust relationship*) with that issuer.

There are several important things to know about an issuer when you establish trust with it:

- What claims does the issuer offer?
- What key should the application use to validate signatures on the issued tokens?
- What URL must users access in order to request a token from the issuer?

Claims can be anything you can imagine, but practically speaking, there are some very common claims offered by most issuers. They tend to be simple, commonly available pieces of information, such as first name, last name, e-mail name, groups and/or roles, and so on. Each issuer can be configured to offer different claims, so the application (technically, this means the architects and developers who design and build the application) needs to know what claims are being offered so they can either select from that list or ask whoever manages the issuer to expand its offering.

All of the questions in the previous list can easily be answered by asking the issuer for *federation metadata*. This is an XML document that the issuer provides to the application. It includes a serialized copy of the issuer's certificate that provides your application with the correct public key to verify incoming tokens. It also includes a list of claims the issuer offers, the URL where users can go to get a token, and other more technical details, such as the token formats that it knows about (although in most cases you'll be using the default SAML format understood by the vast majority of issuers and claims-based applications). WIF includes a wizard that automatically configures your application's identity settings based on this metadata. You just need to give the wizard the URL for the issuer you've selected, and it downloads the metadata and properly configures your application.

STEP 4: CONFIGURE THE ISSUER TO KNOW ABOUT THE APPLICATION

The issuer needs to know a few things about an application before it can issue it any tokens:

- What Uniform Resource Identifier (URI) identifies this application?
- Of the claims that the issuer offers, which ones does this application require and which are optional?
- Should the issuer encrypt the tokens? If so, what key should it use?
- What URL does the application expose in order to receive tokens?

Each application is different, and not all applications need the same claims. One application might need to know the user's groups or roles, while another application might only need a first and last name. So when a client requests a token, part of that request includes an identifier for the application the user is trying to access. This identifier is a URI and, in general, it's simplest to just use the URL of the application, for example, http://www.fabrikam.com/purchasing/.

If you're building a claims-based Web application that has a reasonable degree of security, you'll require the use of SSL (HTTPS) for both the issuer and the application. This will protect the information in the token from eavesdroppers. Applications with stronger security requirements can also request encrypted tokens, in which case, the application typically has its own certificate (and private key). The issuer needs a copy of that certificate (without the private key) in order to encrypt the token issued for that application.

Once again, federation metadata makes this exchange of information easy. WIF includes a tool named FedUtil.exe that generates a federation metadata document for your application, so that you don't have to manually configure the issuer with all of these settings.

◈ *Issuers only provide claims to authorized applications.*

There are, of course, many reasons why an application shouldn't get any more information about a user than it needs. Just two of them are compliance with privacy laws and the design practice of loose coupling.

A Summary of Benefits

To remind you of what you've learned, here's a summary of the benefits that claims can bring you. Claims decouple authentication from authorization so that the application doesn't need to include the logic for a specific mode of authentication. They also decouple roles from authorization logic and allow you to use more finely-grained permissions than roles might provide. You can securely grant access to users who might have previously been inaccessible because they were in different domains, not part of any corporate domain, or using different platforms or technologies.

Finally, you can improve the efficiency of your IT tasks by eliminating duplicate accounts that might span applications or domains and by preventing critical information from becoming stale.

Moving On

Now that you have a general idea of what claims are and how to build a claims-based system, you can go on to the particulars. If you are interested in more details about claims-based architectures for browser-based and smart client-based applications, see the next chapter, "Claims-Based Architectures." If you want to start digging into specifics of how to use claims, start reading the scenarios. Each of the scenarios shows a different situation and demonstrates how to use claims to solve the problem. New concepts are explained within the framework of the scenario to give you a practical understanding of what they mean. You don't need to read the scenarios sequentially, but each chapter presumes that you understand all the material that was explained in earlier chapters.

2 Claims-Based Architectures

The Web is full of interactive applications that users can visit by simply clicking a hyperlink. Once they do, they expect to see the page they want, possibly with a brief stop along the way to log on. Users also expect Web sites to manage their logon sessions, although most of them wouldn't phrase it that way. They would just say that they don't want to retype their password over and over again as they use any of their company's Web applications. For claims to flourish on the Web, it's critical that they support this simple user experience, which is known as single sign-on.

If you've been a part of a Windows domain, you're already familiar with the benefits of single sign-on. You type your password once at the beginning of the day, and that grants you access to a host of resources on the network. Indeed, if you're ever asked to type your password again, you're going to be surprised and annoyed. You've come to expect the transparency provided by Windows Integrated authentication.

Ironically, the popularity of Kerberos has led to its downfall as a flexible, cross-realm solution. Because the domain controller holds the keys to all of the resources in an organization, it's closely guarded by firewalls. If you're away from work, you're expected to use a VPN to access the corporate network. Also, Kerberos is inflexible in terms of the information it provides. It would be nice to extend the Kerberos ticket to include arbitrary claims such as the user's e-mail address, but this isn't a capability that exists right now.

Claims were designed to provide the flexibility that other protocols may not. The possibilities are limited only by your imagination and the policies of your IT department. The standard protocols that exchange claims are specifically designed to cross boundaries such as security realms, firewalls, and different platforms. These protocols were designed by many who wanted to make it easier to securely communicate with each other.

For claims-based applications, single sign-on for the Web is sometimes called *passive federation*.

Claims decouple your applications from the details of identity. It's no longer the application's responsibility to authenticate users. All your application needs is a security token from the issuer that it trusts. Your application won't break if the IT department decides to upgrade security and require users to submit a smart card instead of submitting a user name and password. In addition, it won't need to be recoded, recompiled, or reconfigured.

There's no doubt that domain controllers will continue to guard organizational resources. Also, the business challenges, such as how to resolve issues of trust and how to negotiate legal contracts between companies who want to federate identity, remain. Claims-based identity isn't going to change any of that. However, by layering claims on top of your existing systems, you can remove some of the technical hurdles that may have been impeding your access to a broad, flexible single sign-on solution.

◈ Claims work in conjunction with your existing security systems to broaden their reach and reduce technical obstacles.

A Closer Look at Claims-Based Architectures

There are several architectural approaches you can use to create claims-based applications. For example, Web applications and SOAP Web services each use slightly different techniques, but you'll quickly recognize that the overall shapes of the handshakes are very similar because the goal is always the same: to communicate claims from the issuer to the application in a secure fashion. This chapter shows you how to evaluate the architectures from a variety of perspectives, such as the user experience, the performance implications and optimization opportunities, and how the claims are passed from the issuer to the application. The chapter also offers some advice on how to design your claims and how to know your users.

The goal of many of these architectures is to enable federation with either a browser or a smart client. Federation with a smart client is based on WS-Trust and WS-Federation Active Requestor Profile. These protocols describe the flow of communication between smart clients (such as Windows-based applications) and services (such as WCF services) to request a token from an issuer and then pass that token to the service for authorization.

Federation with a browser is based on WS-Federation Passive Requestor Profile, which describes the same communication flow between the browser and Web applications. It relies on browser redirects, HTTP GET, and POST to request and pass around tokens.

BROWSER-BASED APPLICATIONS

The Microsoft® Windows Identity Foundation (WIF) is a set of .NET Framework classes that allow you to build claims-aware applications. Among other things, it provides the logic you need to process WS-Federation requests. The WS-Federation protocol builds on other standard protocols such as WS-Trust and WS-Security. One of its features is to allow you to request a security token in browser-based applications.

WIF makes claims seem much like forms authentication. If users need to sign in, WIF redirects them to the issuer's logon page. Here, the user is authenticated and is then redirected back to the application. Figure 1 shows the first set of steps that allow someone to use single sign-on with a browser application.

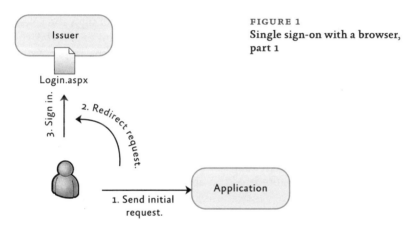

FIGURE 1

Single sign-on with a browser, part 1

If you're familiar with ASP.NET forms authentication, you might assume that the issuer in the preceding figure is using forms authentication because it exposes a page named Login.aspx. But this page may simply be an empty page that is configured in Internet Information Server (IIS) to require Windows Integrated authentication or a client certificate or a smart card. An issuer should be configured to use the most natural and secure method of authentication for the users that sign in there. Sometimes a simple user name and password form is enough, but obviously this requires some interaction and slows down the user. Windows Integrated authentication is easier and more secure for employees in the same domain as the issuer.

When the user is redirected to the issuer's log-on page, several query string arguments are passed that act as instructions to the issuer. Here are two of the key arguments with example values:

wa=wsignin1.0

> The **wa** argument stands for "action," and says one of two things—whether you're logging on (wsignin1.0) or logging off (wsignout1.0).

wtrealm=http://www.fabrikam.com/purchasing/

> The **wtrealm** argument stands for "target realm" and contains a Uniform Resource Indicator (URI) that identifies the application. The issuer uses the URI to identify the application the user is logging on to. The URI also allows the issuer to perform other tasks, such as associating the claims for the application and replying to addresses.

The issuer is told which application is in use so that it issues only the claims that the application needs.

After the issuer authenticates the user, it gathers whatever claims the application needs (using the **wtrealm** parameter to identify the target application), packages them into a security token, and signs the token with its private key. If the application wants its tokens encrypted, the issuer encrypts the token with the public key in the application's certificate.

Now the issuer asks the browser to go back to the application. The browser sends the token to the application so it can process the claims. Once this is done, the user can begin using the application.

To accomplish this, the issuer returns an HTML page to the browser, including a **<form>** element with the form-encoded token inside. The form's **action** attribute is set to submit the token to whatever URL was configured for the application. The user doesn't normally see this form because the issuer also emits a bit of JavaScript that auto-posts it. If scripts are disabled, the user will need to click a button to post the response to the server. Figure 2 shows this process.

If this sounds familiar, it's because forms authentication uses a similar redirection technique with the **ReturnURL** parameter.

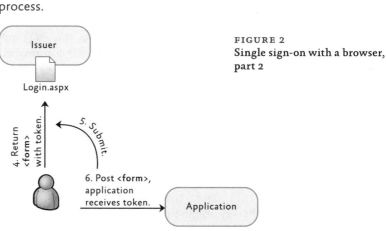

FIGURE 2
Single sign-on with a browser, part 2

7. WIF validates token and issues a cookie.
8. WIF presents the claims to the application.
9. Application process claims and continues.

Now consider this process from the user's experience. If the issuer uses Windows Integrated authentication, the user clicks the link to the application, waits for a moment while the browser is first redirected to the issuer and then back to the application, and then the user is logged on without any additional input. If the issuer requires input from the user, such as a user name and password form or a smart card, users have a brief pause to log on, and then they can use the application. From the user's point of view, the logon process with claims is the same as what he or she is to, which is critical.

Understanding the Sequence of Steps

The steps illustrated in the preceding illustrations can also be depicted as a sequence of steps that occur over time. Figure 3 shows this sequence.

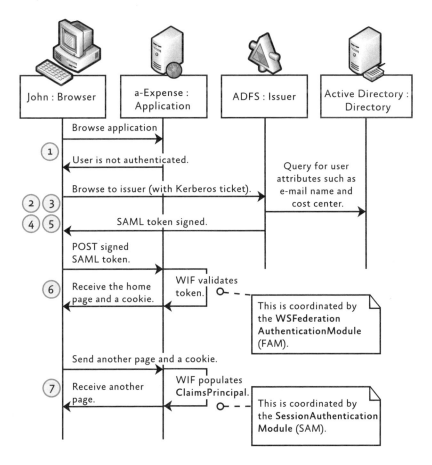

FIGURE 3
Browser-based message sequence

If a user is not authenticated, the browser requests a token from the issuer, which in this case is Active Directory Federation Services (ADFS). ADFS queries Active Directory for the necessary attributes and returns a signed token to the browser.

After the POST arrives at the application, WIF takes over. The application has configured a WIF HTTP module, named **WSFedera-**

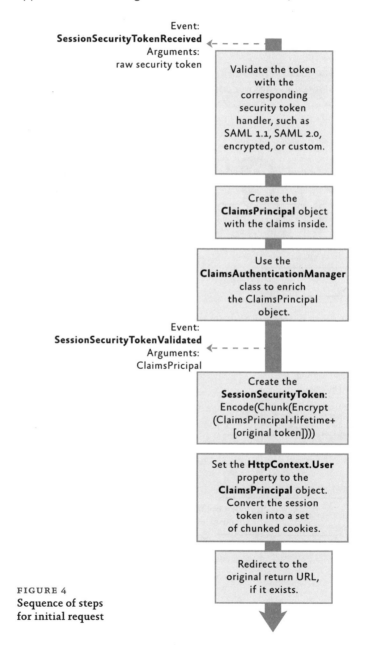

Event:
SessionSecurityTokenReceived
Arguments:
raw security token

Validate the token with the corresponding security token handler, such as SAML 1.1, SAML 2.0, encrypted, or custom.

Create the **ClaimsPrincipal** object with the claims inside.

Use the **ClaimsAuthenticationManager** class to enrich the ClaimsPrincipal object.

Event:
SessionSecurityTokenValidated
Arguments:
ClaimsPricipal

Create the **SessionSecurityToken**: Encode(Chunk(Encrypt (ClaimsPrincipal+lifetime+ [original token])))

Set the **HttpContext.User** property to the **ClaimsPrincipal** object. Convert the session token into a set of chunked cookies.

Redirect to the original return URL, if it exists.

FIGURE 4
Sequence of steps for initial request

tionAuthenticationModule (FAM), to intercept this POST to the application and handle the processing of the token. The FAM listens for the **AuthenticateRequest** event. The event handler performs several validation steps, including checking the token's audience restriction and the expiration date. Audience restriction is defined by the **AudienceURI** element. It determines the URIs the application can accept in the token. The FAM also uses the issuer's public key to make sure that the token was signed by the trusted issuer and was not modified in transit. Then it parses the claims in the token and uses the **HttpContext.User.Identity** property (or equivalently the **Page.User** property) to present an **IClaimsPrincipal** object to the application. It also issues a cookie to begin a logon session, just like what would happen if you were using forms authentication instead of claims. This means that the authentication process isn't repeated until the user signs off or otherwise destroys the cookie or until the session expires (sessions are typically designed to last for a single work day).

Figure 4 shows the steps that WIF takes for the initial request, when the application receives a token from the issuer.

One of the steps that the FAM performs is to create the session token. On the wire, this translates into a sequence of cookies named **FedAuth[n]**. These cookies are the result of compressing, encrypting, and encoding the **ClaimsPrincipal** object, along with any other attributes. The cookies are chunked to avoid overstepping any size limitations.

Figure 5 shows what the network traffic looks like for the initial request.

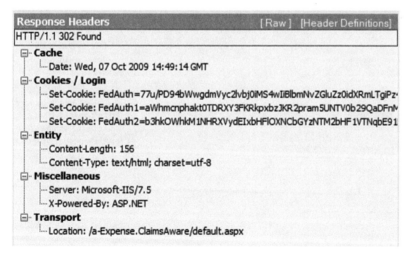

FIGURE 5
Sequence of cookies

On subsequent requests to the application, the **SessionAuthen-ticationModule** intercepts the cookies and uses them to reconstruct the **ClaimsPrincipal** object. Figure 6 shows the steps that WIF takes for any subsequent requests.

FIGURE 6
Steps for subsequent requests

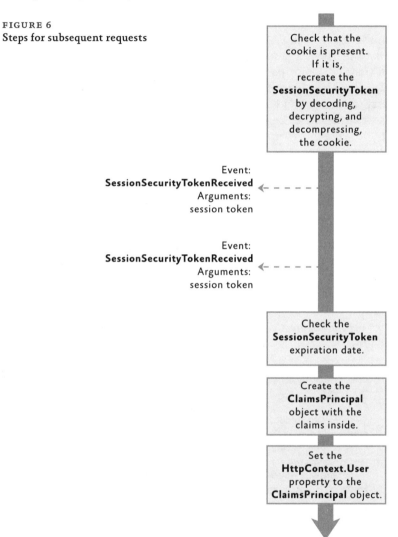

Check that the cookie is present. If it is, recreate the **SessionSecurityToken** by decoding, decrypting, and decompressing, the cookie.

Event:
SessionSecurityTokenReceived
Arguments:
session token

Event:
SessionSecurityTokenReceived
Arguments:
session token

Check the **SessionSecurityToken** expiration date.

Create the **ClaimsPrincipal** object with the claims inside.

Set the **HttpContext.User** property to the **ClaimsPrincipal** object.

Figure 7 shows what the network traffic looks like for subsequent requests.

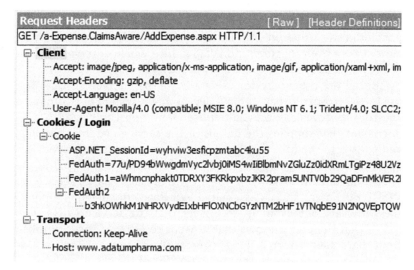

All of the steps, both for the initial and subsequent requests, should run over the Secure Sockets Layer (SSL) to ensure that an eavesdropper can't steal either the token or the logon session cookie and replay them to the application in order to impersonate a legitimate user.

Optimizing Performance

Are there opportunities for performance optimizations here? The answer is a definite "Yes." You can use the logon session cookie to cache some state on the client to reduce round-trips to the issuer. The issuer also issues its own cookie so that users remain logged on at the issuer and can access many applications. Think about how this works—when a user visits a second application and that application redirects back to the same issuer, the issuer sees its cookie and knows the user has recently been authenticated, so it can immediately issue a token without having to authenticate again. This is how to use claims to achieve Internet-friendly single sign-on with a browser-based application.

Applications and issuers use cookies to achieve Internet-friendly single-sign on.

SMART CLIENTS

When you use a Web service, you don't use a browser. Instead, you use an arbitrary client application that includes logic for handling claims-based identity protocols. There are two protocols that are important in this situation: WS-Trust, which describes how to get a security token from an issuer, and WS-Security, which describes how to pass that security token to a claims-based Web service.

Recall the procedure for using a SOAP-based Web service. You use the Microsoft Visual Studio® development system or a command line tool to download a Web Service Definition Language (WSDL) document that supplies the details of the service's address, binding, and contract. The tool then generates a proxy and updates your application's configuration file with the information discovered in the WSDL document. When you do this with a claims-based service, its WSDL document and its associated WS-Policy document supply all the necessary details about the issuer that the service trusts. This means that the proxy knows that it needs to obtain a security token from that issuer before making requests to the service. Because this information is stored in the configuration file of the client application, at run time the proxy can get that token before talking to the service. This optimizes the handshake a bit compared to the browser scenario, because the browser had to visit the application first before being redirected to the issuer. Figure 8 shows the sequence of steps for smart clients.

The steps for a smart client are similar to those for browser-based applications. The smart client makes a round-trip to the issuer, using WS-Trust to request a security token. In step 1, The Orders Web service is configured with the **WSFederationHttpBinding**. This binding specifies a Web service policy that obligates the client to attach a SAML token to the security header to successfully invoke the Web service. This means that the client will first have to call the issuer with a set of credentials such as a user name and password to get a SAML token back. In step 2, the client can call the Web service with the token attached to the security header.

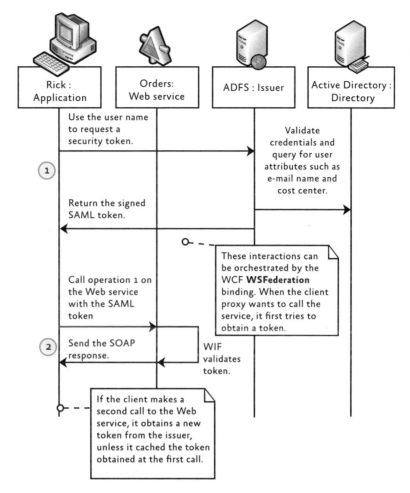

1 Use the user name to request a security token.

Validate credentials and query for user attributes such as e-mail name and cost center.

Return the signed SAML token.

These interactions can be orchestrated by the WCF **WSFederation** binding. When the client proxy wants to call the service, it first tries to obtain a token.

Call operation 1 on the Web service with the SAML token

2 Send the SOAP response.

WIF validates token.

If the client makes a second call to the Web service, it obtains a new token from the issuer, unless it cached the token obtained at the first call.

FIGURE 8
Smart client-based message sequence

Rick : Application

Orders: Web service

ADFS : Issuer

Active Directory : Directory

Figure 9 shows a trace of the messages that occur in the smart client scenario.

Action	From/To
http://docs.oasis-open.org/ws-sx/ws-trust/200512/RST/Issue	https://login.adatumpharma.com/adfs/services/trust/13/usernamemixed
http://docs.oasis-open.org/ws-sx/ws-trust/200512/RSTRC/IssueFinal	
http://tempuri.org/GetOrders	
http://tempuri.org/GetOrdersResponse	http://orders.adatumpharma.com/Orders.svc

FIGURE 9
Smart client network traffic

The WS-Trust request (technically named a Request for Security Token, or RST for short) includes a field named **AppliesTo**, which allows the smart client to indicate a URI for the Web service it's ultimately trying to access. This is similar to the **wtrealm** query string argument used in the case of a Web browser. Once the issuer authenticates the user, it knows which application wants access and it can decide which claims to issue. Then the issuer sends back the response (RSTR), which includes a signed security token that is encrypted with the public key of the Web service. The token includes a *proof key*. This is a symmetric key randomly generated by the issuer and included as part of the RSTR so that the client also gets a copy.

Now it's up to the client to send the token to the Web service in the **<Security>** header of the SOAP envelope. The client must sign the SOAP headers (one of which is a time stamp) with the proof key to show that it knows the key. This extra cryptographic evidence further assures the Web service that the caller was, indeed, the one who was issued the token in the first place.

At this point, it's typical to start a session using the **WS-Secure-Conversation** protocol. The client will probably cache the RSTR for up to a day in case it needs to reconnect to the same service later on.

Federating Identity Across Realms

So far you've learned enough about claims-based identity to understand how to design and build a claims-based application where the issuer directly authenticates the users.

But you can take this one step further. You can expand your issuer's capabilities to accept a security token from another issuer, instead of requiring the user to authenticate directly. Your issuer now not only issues security tokens, but it also accepts tokens from other issuers that it trusts. This enables you to federate identity with other realms (these are separate security domains), which is truly a powerful feature. Much of the federation process is actually accomplished by your IT staff, because it depends on how issuers are configured. But it's important to be aware of these possibilities because, ultimately, they lead to more features for your application, even though you might not have to change your application in any way. Also, some of these possibilities may have implications for your application's design.

THE BENEFITS OF CROSS-REALM IDENTITY

Maintaining an identity database for users can be a daunting task. Even something as simple as a database that holds user names and passwords can be painful to manage. Users forget their passwords on a regular basis, and the security stance taken by your company may not allow you to simply e-mail forgotten passwords to them the way many low-security Web sites do. If maintaining a database for users inside your enterprise is difficult, imagine doing this for hundreds or thousands remote users.

Managing a role database for remote users is just as difficult. Imagine Alice, who works for a partner company and uses your purchasing application. On the day that your IT staff provisioned her account, she worked in the purchasing department, so the IT staff assigned her the role of Purchaser, which granted her permission to use the application. But because she works for a different company, how is your company going to find out when she transfers to the Sales department? Or what if she quits? In both cases, you'd want to know about her change of status, but it's unlikely that anyone in the HR department at her company is going to notify you.

Alice's identity is an asset of Alice's organization so her company should manage it. Also, storing information about remote users can be looked at as a liability for your company.

It's unavoidable that any data you store about a remote user eventually becomes stale. How can you safely expose an application for a partner business to use?

One of the most powerful features of claims-based identity is that you can decentralize it. Instead of having your issuer authenticate remote users directly, set up a trust relationship with an issuer that belongs to the other company. This means that your issuer trusts their issuer to authenticate users in their realm. Their employees are happy because they don't need special credentials to use your application. They use the same single sign-on mechanism they've always used in their company. Your application still works because it continues to get the same boarding pass it needs. The claims you get in your boarding pass for these remote users might include less powerful roles because they aren't employees of your company, but your issuer will be responsible for determining the proper assignments. Finally, your application doesn't need to change when a new organization becomes a partner. The fan-out of issuers to applications is a real benefit of using claims—you reconfigure one issuer and many downstream applications become accessible to many new users.

◈ Claims can be used to decentralize identity, eliminating stale data about remote users.

Another benefit is that claims allow you to logically store data about users. Data can be kept in the store that is authoritative rather than in a store that is simply convenient to use or easily accessible.

Identity federation removes hurdles that may have stopped you from opening the doors to new users. Once your company decides which realms should be allowed access to your claims-based application, your IT staff can set up the proper trust relationships. Then you can, for example, invite employees from a company that uses Java, to access your application without having to issue passwords for each of them. They only need a Java-based issuer, and those have been available for years. Another possibility is to federate identity with Windows Live™, which supports claims-based identity. This means that anyone with a Windows Live ID can use your application.

HOW FEDERATED IDENTITY WORKS

You've already seen how federated identity works within a single realm. Indeed, Figure 2 is a small example of identity federation between your application and a local issuer in your realm. That relationship doesn't change when your issuer federates with an issuer in a different realm. The only change is that your issuer is now configured to accept a security token issued by a partner company instead of directly authenticating users from that company. Your issuer trusts another issuer to authenticate users so it doesn't have to. This is similar to how your application trusts its issuer.

Figure 10 shows the steps for federating identity across realms.

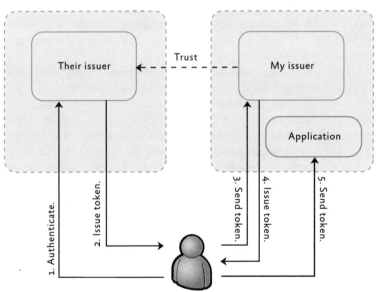

FIGURE 10
Federating identity across realms

This is exactly the same as what you've already seen in the first illustration in this chapter, with the addition of an initial handshake in the partner's realm. Users first authenticate with an issuer in their own realm. They present the tokens they receive from their exchanges to your issuer, which accepts it in lieu of authenticating them directly. Your issuer can now issue a token for your application to use. This token is what the user sends to your application. (Of course, users know nothing about this protocol—it's actually the browser or smart client that does this on their behalf). Remember, your application will only accept tokens signed by the one issuer that it trusts. Remote users won't get access if they try to send a token from their local issuer to your application.

At this point, you may be thinking, "Why should my company trust some other company to authenticate people that use my application? That doesn't seem safe!" Think about how this works *without* claims-based identity. Executives from both companies meet and sign legal contracts. Then the IT staff from the partner company contacts your IT staff and specifies which of their users need accounts provisioned and which roles they will need. The legal contracts help ensure that nobody abuses the trust that's been established. This process has been working for years and is an accepted practice.

Another question is why should you bother provisioning accounts for those remote users when you know that data will get stale over time? All that claims-based identity does is help you *automate the trust*, so that you get fresh information each time a user visits your application. If Alice quits, the IT staff at her company has great personal incentive to disable her account quickly. They don't want a potentially disgruntled employee to have access to company resources. That means that Alice won't be able to authenticate with their issuer anymore, which means she won't be able to use your application, either. Notice that nobody needed to call you up to tell you about Alice. By decentralizing identity management, you get better information (authoritative information, you could say) about remote users in a timely fashion.

One possible drawback of federating identity with many other companies is that your issuer becomes a single point of failure for all of your federation relationships. Issuers should be as tightly guarded as domain controllers. Adding features is never without risk, but the rewards can lead to lower costs, better security, simpler applications, and happier users.

I think of an issuer as an "identity transformer." It converts incoming identities into something that's intelligible to the application.

◈ *ADFS uses a rules engine to support claims transformation.*

Identity Transformation

The issuer's job is to take some generic incoming identity (perhaps from a Kerberos ticket or an X.509 certificate) and transform it into a security token that your application can use. That security token is like the boarding pass, in that it contains all of the user's identity details that your application needs to do its job, and nothing more. Perhaps instead of the user's Windows groups, your boarding pass contains roles that you can use right away.

On the other end of the protocol are users who can use their single sign-on credentials to access many applications because the issuer in their realm knows how to authenticate them. Their local issuer provides claims to applications in their local realm as well as to issuers in other realms so that they can use many applications, both local and remote, without having to remember special credentials for each one.

Consider the application's local issuer in the last illustration, "Federating identity across realms." It receives a security token from a user in some other realm. Its first job is to reject the request if the incoming token wasn't issued by one of the select issuers that it trusts. But once that check is out of the way, its job now becomes one of *claims transformation*. It must transform the claims made by the remote issuer into claims that make sense for your application. For a practical example, see chapter 4, "Federated Identity for Web Applications."

In ADFS, this sort of transformation is done with rules such as, "If you see a claim of this type, with this value, issue this claim instead." For example, your application may have a role called Managers that grants special access to manager-specific features. That claim may map directly onto a Managers group in your realm, so that local users who are in the Managers group always get the Managers role in your application. In the partner's realm, they may have a group called Supervisors that needs to access the manager-specific features in your application. The transformation from Supervisors to Managers can happen in their issuer; if it does not, it must happen in yours. This transformation simply requires another rule in ADFS. The point is that issuers such as ADFS are specifically designed to support this type of transformation, because it's rare that two companies will use exactly the same vocabulary.

HOME REALM DISCOVERY

Now that you've seen the possibility of cross-realm federation, think about how it works with browser-based applications. Here are the steps:

1. Alice (in a remote realm) clicks a link to your application.

2. You redirect Alice to your local issuer, just like before.

3. Your issuer redirects Alice's browser to the issuer in her realm.

4. Alice's local issuer authenticates and issues a token, sending Alice's browser back to your issuer with that token.

5. Your issuer validates the token, transforms the claims, and issues a token for your application to use.

6. Your issuer sends Alice's browser back to your application, with the token that contains the claims your application needs.

The mystery here is in step 3. How does the issuer know that Alice is from a remote realm? What prevents the issuer from thinking she's a local user and trying to authenticate her directly, which will only fail and frustrate the user? Even if the issuer knew that Alice was from a remote realm, how would it know which realm it was? This is because it's likely that you'll have more than one partner.

This problem is known as "home realm discovery." Your issuer has to determine if Alice is from the local realm or if she's from some partner organization. If she's local, the issuer can authenticate her directly. If she's remote, the issuer needs to know a URL to redirect her to so that she can be authenticated by her home realm's issuer.

There are two ways to solve this problem. The simplest one is to have the user help out. In step 2, when Alice's browser is redirected to your local ADFS, it pauses the protocol and displays a Web page to Alice, asking her what company she works for. (Note that it doesn't help Alice to lie about this, because her credentials are only good for one of the companies on the list—her company.) Alice clicks the link for her company and the protocol continues, since the issuer now knows what to do. To avoid asking Alice this question in the future, your issuer sets a cookie in her browser so that next time it'll know who her issuer is without having to ask.

Take a look at chapter 3, "Claims-Based Single Sign-On for the Web," to see an example of this technique.

The second way to solve this problem is by adding a hint to the query string that's in the link that Alice clicks in step 1. That query string will contain a parameter named **whr** (**hr** stands for home realm).

The issuer (ADFS 2.0) looks for this hint and automatically maps it to the URL of the user's home realm. This means that the issuer doesn't have to ask Alice who her issuer is because the application relays that information to the issuer. The issuer uses a cookie, just as before, to ensure that Alice is never bothered with this question.

Home Realm Discovery and Web Services

Using a Web page to get the user's help may make sense for Web applications. They are interactive by nature and the browser can display a home realm discovery page if needed. But how do you solve this problem with smart clients and Web services? This is where information cards can help (note that information cards are beyond the scope of this guide).

Design Considerations for Claims-Based Applications

Admittedly, it's difficult to offer general prescriptive guidance for designing claims because they are so dependent on the particular application. This section poses a series of questions and offers some approaches to consider as you look at your options.

WHAT MAKES A GOOD CLAIM?

Like many of the most important design decisions, this question doesn't always have a clear answer. What's important is that you understand the tensions at play and the tradeoffs you're facing. Here are some concrete examples that might help you start thinking about some general criteria for what makes a good claim.

> My IT people make sure that the links to remote applications always include this information. It makes the application much friendlier for the user and protects the privacy of my company by not revealing all of its partners.

First, consider a user's e-mail address. That's a prime candidate for a claim in almost any system, because it's generally very tightly coupled to the user's identity, and it's something that everyone needs if you decide to federate identity across realms. An e-mail name can help you personalize your system for the user in a very meaningful way.

What about a user's choice of a skin or theme for your Web site? Certainly, this is "personalization" data, but it's also data that's particular to a single application, and it's hard to argue that this is part of a user's identity. Your application should manage this locally.

> Take a look at chapter 4, "Federated Identity for Web Applications," to see an example of this technique.

What about a user's permission to access data in your application? While it may make sense in some systems to model permissions as claims, it's easy to end up with an overwhelming number of these claims as you model finer and finer levels of authorization. A better approach is to define a boundary that separates the authorization data you'll get from claims from the data you'll handle through other means. For example, in cross-realm federation scenarios, it can be beneficial to allow other realms to be authoritative for some high-level roles. Your application can then map those roles onto fine-grained permissions with tools such as Windows Authorization Manager (AzMan). But unless you've got an issuer that's specifically designed for managing fine-grained permissions, it's probably best to keep your claims at a much higher level.

Before making any attribute into a claim, ask yourself the following questions:

- Is this data a core part of how I model user identity?
- Is the issuer an authority on this information?
- Will this data be used by more than one application?
- Do I want an issuer to manage this data or should my application manage it directly?

HOW CAN YOU UNIQUELY IDENTIFY ONE USER FROM ANOTHER?

Because each person isn't born with a unique identifier (indeed, most people treasure their privacy), this has always been, and will likely always be a tricky problem. Claims don't make this any easier. Fortunately, not all applications need to know exactly who the user is. Simply being able to identify one returning user from another is enough to implement a shopping cart, for example. Many applications don't even need to go this far. But other applications have per-user state that they need to track, so they require a unique identifier for each user.

Traditional applications typically rely on a user's sign-in name to distinguish one user from the next. So what happens when you start building claims-based applications and you give up control over authentication? You'll need to pick one (or a combination of multiple) claims to uniquely identify your user, and you'll need to rely on your issuer to give you the same values for each of those claims every time that user visits your application. It might make sense to ask the issuer to give you a claim that represents a unique identifier for the user. This can be tricky in a cross-realm federation scenario, where more than one issuer is involved. In these more complicated scenarios, it helps to remember that each issuer has a URI that identifies it and that can be used to scope any identifier that it issues for a user. An example of such a URI is http://issuer.fabrikam.com/unique-user-id-assigned-from-fabrikams-realm.

E-mail addresses have convenient properties of uniqueness and scope already built in, so you might choose to use an e-mail claim as a unique identifier for the user. If you do, you'll need to plan ahead if you want users to be able to change the e-mail addresses associated with their data. You'll also need a way to associate a new e-mail address with that data.

HOW CAN YOU GET A LIST OF ALL POSSIBLE USERS AND ALL POSSIBLE CLAIMS?

One thing that's important to keep in mind when you build a claims-based application is that you're never going to know about all the users that could use your application. You've given up that control in exchange for less responsibility, worry, and hassle over programming against any one particular user store. Users just appear at your doorstep, presenting the token they got from the issuer that you trust. That token gives you information about who they are and what they can do. In addition, tokens that contain the necessary claims should be rejected, even if they come from a trusted source. If you've designed things properly, you're not going to have to change your code to support new users, even if those users come from other realms, as they do in federation scenarios.

So how can you build a list of users that allows administrators to choose which users have permission to access your application and which don't? The answer is, "Find another way!" This is a perfect example of where an issuer should be involved with authorization decisions. The issuer shouldn't issue tokens to users who aren't privileged enough to use your application. It should be configured to do this without you having to do anything at all in your application.

When designing a claims-based application, always keep in mind that a certain amount of responsibility for identity has been lifted from your shoulders as an application developer. If an identity-related task feels hard or impossible to build into your application logic, consider whether it's possible for your issuer to handle that task for you.

WHERE SHOULD CLAIMS BE ISSUED?

This question is a moot point when you have a simple system with only one issuer. But when you have more complicated systems where multiple issuers are chained into a path of trust that leads from the application back to the issuer in the user's home realm, this question becomes very relevant.

❧ *Always get claims from authoritative sources.*

The short answer to the question is: "Use the issuer that knows best."

Take, for example, a claim such as a person's e-mail name. The e-mail name of a user isn't going to change depending on which application he or she uses. It makes sense for this type of claim to be issued close to the user's home realm. Indeed, it's most likely that the first issuer in the chain, which is the identity provider, would be authoritative for the user's e-mail name. This means that downstream issuers and applications can benefit from that central claim. If the e-mail name is ever updated, it only needs to be updated at that central location.

Now think about an "action" claim, which is specific to an application. An application for expense reporting might want to allow or disallow actions such as **submitExpenseReport** and **approveExpenseReport**. Another type of application, such as one that tracks bugs, would have very different actions, such as **reportBug** and **assignBug**.

In some systems, you might find that it works best to have the individual applications handle these applications internally, based on higher-level claims such as roles or groups. But if you do decide to factor these actions out into claims, it would be best to have an issuer close to the application be authoritative for them. Having local authority over these sorts of claims means you can more quickly implement policy changes without having to contact some central authority.

What about a group claim or a role claim? In traditional RBAC (Role-Based Access Control) systems, a user is assigned to one or more groups, the groups are mapped to roles, and roles are mapped to actions. There are many reasons why this is good: the mapping from roles to actions for an application can be done by someone who is familiar with it and who understands the actions defined for that application. For example, the mapping from user to groups can be done by a central administrator who knows the semantics of each group. Also, while groups can be managed in a central store, roles and actions can be more decentralized and handled by the various departments and product groups that define them. This allows for a much more agile system where identity and authorization data can be centralized or decentralized as needed.

Issuers are typically placed at boundaries in organizations. Take, for example, a company with several departments. Each department might have its own issuer, while the company has a central issuer that acts as a gateway for claims that enter or leave it. If a user at this company accesses an application in another, similarly structured company, the request will end up being processed by four issuers:

Issuers are typically found at organizational boundaries.

- The departmental issuer, which authenticates the user and supplies an e-mail name and some initial group claims
- The company's central issuer, which adds more groups and some roles based on those groups
- The application's central issuer, which maps roles from the user's company to roles that the application's company understands (this issuer may also add additional role-claims based on the ones already present)
- The application's departmental issuer, which maps roles onto actions

You can see that as the request crosses each of these boundaries, the issuers there enrich and filter the user's security context by issuing claims that make sense for the target context, based on its requirements and the privacy policies. Is the e-mail name passed all the way through to the application? That depends on whether the user's company trusts the application's company with that information, and whether the application's company thinks the application needs to know that information.

3 Claims-Based Single Sign-On for the Web

This chapter walks you through an example of single sign-on (SSO) for intranet and extranet Web users who all belong to a single security realm. You'll see examples of two existing applications that become claims-aware. One of the applications uses forms authentication, and one uses Windows authentication. Once the applications use claims-based authentication, you'll see how it's possible to interact with the applications either from the company's internal network or from the public Internet.

This basic scenario doesn't show how to establish trust relationships across enterprises. (That is discussed in chapter 4, "Federated Identity for Web Applications.") It focuses on how to implement single sign-on and single sign-off within a security domain as a preparation for sharing resources with other security domains, and how to migrate applications to Microsoft® Windows® Azure. In short, this scenario contains the commonly used elements that will appear in all claims-aware applications.

❧ *For SSO, the issuer also creates a session with the user that works with different applications.*

The Premise

Adatum is a medium-sized company that uses Microsoft Active Directory® directory service to authenticate the employees in its corporate network. Adatum's sales force uses a-Order, Adatum's order processing system, to enter, process, and manage customer orders. Adatum employees also use aExpense, an expense tracking and reimbursement system for business-related expenses.

Both applications are built with ASP.NET 3.5 and are deployed in Adatum's data center. Figure 1 shows a whiteboard diagram that shows the structure of a-Order and a-Expense.

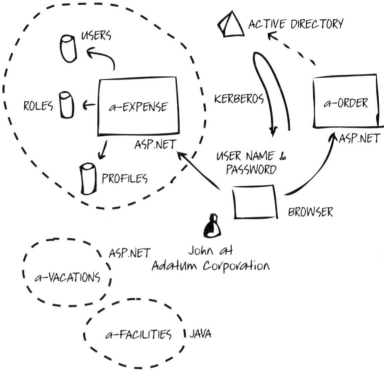

FIGURE 1
Adatum infrastructure before claims

The two applications handle authentication differently. The a-Order application uses Windows authentication. It recognizes the credentials used when employees logged on to the corporate network. The application doesn't need to prompt them for user names and passwords. For authorization, a-Order uses roles that are derived from groups stored in Active Directory. In this way, a-Order is integrated into the Adatum infrastructure.

The user experience for a-Expense is a bit more complicated. The a-Expense application uses its own authentication, authorization, and user profile information. This data is stored in custom tables in an application database. Users enter a user name and password in a Web form whenever they start the application. The a-Expense application's authentication approach reflects its history. The application began as a Human Resources project that was developed outside of Adatum's IT department. Over time, other departments adopted it. Now it's a part of Adatum's corporate IT solution.

The a-Expense access control rules use application-specific roles. Access control is intermixed with the application's business logic.

Keeping the user database for forms-based authentication up to date is painful since it isn't integrated into Adatum's process for managing employee accounts.

Some of the user profile information that a-Expense uses also exists in Active Directory, but because a-Expense isn't integrated with the corporate enterprise directory, it can't access it. For example, Active Directory contains each employee's cost center, which is also one of the pieces of information maintained in the a-Expense user profile database. Changing a user's cost center in a-Expense is messy and error prone. All employees have to manually update their profiles when their cost centers change.

Goals and Requirements

Adatum has a number of goals in moving to a claims-based identity solution. One goal is to add the single sign-on capability to its network. This allows employees to log on once and then be able to access all authorized systems, including a-Expense. With SSO, users will not have to enter a user name and password when they use a-Expense.

A second goal is to enable Adatum employees to access corporate applications from the Internet. Members of the sales force often travel to customer sites and need to be able to use a-Expense and aOrder without the overhead of establishing a virtual private network (VPN) session.

A third goal is to plan for the future. Adatum wants a flexible solution that it can adapt as the company grows and changes. Right now, a priority is to implement an architecture that allows them to host some applications in a cloud environment such as Windows Azure. Moving operations out of their data center will reduce their capital expenditures and make it simpler to manage the applications. Adatum is also considering giving their customers access to some applications, such as a-Order. Adatum knows that claims-based identity and access control are the foundations needed to enable these plans.

While meeting these goals, Adatum wants to make sure its solution reuses its existing investment in its enterprise directory. The company wants to make sure user identities remain under central administrative control and don't span multiple stores. Nonetheless, Adatum wants its business units to have the flexibility to control access to the data they manage. For example, not everyone at Adatum is authorized to use the a-Expense application. Currently, access to the program is controlled by application-specific roles stored in a departmentally administered database. Adatum's identity solution must preserve this flexibility.

Finally, Adatum also wants its identity solution to work with multiple platforms and vendors. And, like all companies, Adatum wants to ensure that any Internet access to corporate applications is secure.

Your choice of an identity solution should be based on clear goals and requirements.

Dealing with change is one of the challenges of IT operations.

With these considerations in mind, Adatum's technical staff has made the decision to modify both the aExpense and the a-Order applications to support claims-based single sign-on.

Overview of the Solution

Claims can take advantage of existing directory information.

Nobody likes changing their Active Directory schema. Adding app-specific rules or claims from a non–Active Directory data store to a claims issuer is easier.

The first step was to analyze which pieces of identity information were common throughout the company and which were specific to particular applications. The idea was to make maximum use of the existing investment in directory information. Upon review, Adatum discovered that their Active Directory store already contained the necessary information. In particular, the enterprise directory maintained user names and passwords, given names and surnames, e-mail addresses, employee cost centers, office locations, and telephone numbers.

Since this information was already in Active Directory, the claims-based identity solution would not require changing the Active Directory schema to suit any specific application.

They determined that the main change would be to introduce an issuer of claims for the organization. Adatum's applications will trust this issuer to authenticate users.

Adatum envisions that, over time, all of its applications will eventually trust the issuer. Since information about employees is a corporate asset, the eventual goal is for no application to maintain a custom employee database. Adatum recognizes that some applications have specialized user profile information that will not (and should not) be moved to the enterprise directory. Adatum wants to avoid adding application-specific attributes to its Active Directory store, and it wants to keep management as decentralized as possible.

For the initial rollout, the company decided to focus on a-Expense and a-Order. The a-Order application only needs configuration changes that allow it to use Active Directory groups and users as claims. Although there is no immediate difference in the application's structure or functionality, this change will set the stage for eventually allowing external partners to access.

The a-Expense application will continue to use its own application-specific roles database, but the rest of the user attributes will come from claims that the issuer provides. This will provide single sign-on for aExpense users, streamline the management of user identities, and allow the application to be reachable remotely from the Internet.

Note: *You might ask why Adatum chose claims-based identity for a-Expense rather than Windows authentication. Like claims, Windows authentication provides SSO, and it is a simpler solution than issuing claims and configuring the application to process claims.*

There's no disagreement here: Windows authentication is extremely well suited for intranet SSO and should be used when that is the only requirement.

Adatum's goals are broader than just SSO, however. Adatum wants its employees to have remote access to a-Expense and a-Order without requiring a VPN connection. Also, Adatum wants to move aExpense to Windows Azure and eventually allow customers to view their pending orders in the aOrder application over the Internet. The claims-based approach is best suited to these scenarios.

Staging is helpful. You can change authentication first without affecting authorization.

Figure 2 shows the proposal, as it was presented on Adatum's whiteboards by the technical staff. The diagram shows how internal users will be authenticated.

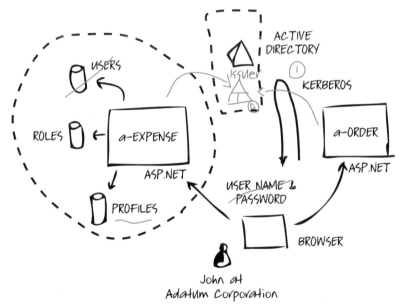

FIGURE 2
Moving to claims-based identity

This claims-based architecture allows Adatum employees to work from home just by publishing the application and the issuer through the firewall and proxies. Figure 3 shows the way Adatum employees can use the corporate intranet from home.

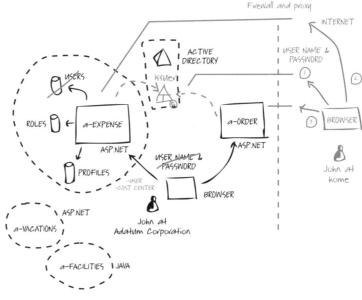

FIGURE 3
Claims-based identity over the Internet

Once the issuer establishes the remote user's identity by prompting for a user name and password, the same claims are sent to the application, just as if the employee is inside the corporate firewall.

This solution makes Adatum's authentication strategy much more flexible. For example, Adatum could ask for additional authentication requirements when someone connects from the Internet, such as smart cards, PINs, or even biometric data. Because authentication is now the responsibility of the issuer, and the applications always receive the same set of claims, the applications don't need to be rewritten. The ability to change the way you authenticate users without having to change your applications is a real benefit of using claims.

You can also look at this proposed architecture from the point of view of the HTTP message stream. For more information, see the message sequence diagrams in chapter 2, "Claims-Based Architectures."

Inside the Implementation

Now is a good time to walk through the process of converting a-Expense into a claims-aware application in more detail. As you go through this section, you may want to download the Visual Studio® solution 1SingleSignOn from http://claimsid.codeplex.com. This solution contains implementations of a-Expense and a-Order, with and without claims. If you are not interested in the mechanics, you should skip to the next section.

A-EXPENSE BEFORE CLAIMS

Before claims, the a-Expense application used forms authentication to establish user identity. It's worth taking a moment to review the process of forms authentication so that the differences with the claims-aware version are easier to see. In simple terms, forms authentication consists of a credentials database and an HTTP redirect to a logon page.

Figure 4 shows the a-Expense application with forms authentication.

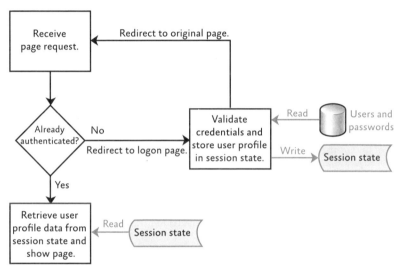

Many Web applications store user profile information in cookies rather than in the session state because cookies scale better on the server side. Scale wasn't a concern here because a-Expense is a departmental application.

FIGURE 4
a-Expense with forms authentication

The logon page serves two purposes in a-Expense. It authenticates the user by asking for credentials that are then checked against the password database, and it also copies application-specific user profile information into the ASP.NET's session state object for later use. Examples of profile information are the user's full name, cost center, and assigned roles. The a-Expense application keeps its user profile information in the same database as user passwords, which is typical for applications that use forms authentication.

a-Order uses session state, but cookies scale better on the server side. a-Order is a departmental app with a small number of simultaneous users.

> **Note:** *a-Expense intentionally uses custom code for authentication, authorization, and profiles instead of using Membership, Roles, and Profile providers. This is typical of legacy applications that might have been written before ASP.NET 2.0.*

In ASP.NET, adding forms authentication to a Web application has three parts: an annotation in the application's Web.config file to enable forms authentication, a logon page that asks for credentials, and a handler method that validates those credentials against application data. Here is how those pieces work.

The Web.config file for a-Expense enables forms authentication with the following XML declarations:

```xml
<authentication mode="Forms">
    <forms loginUrl="~/login.aspx"
           requireSSL="true" ... />
</authentication>

<authorization>
    <deny users="?" />
</authorization>
```

The **authentication** element tells the ASP.NET runtime (or Internet Information Services, IIS, 7.0 when running both in ASP.NET integrated mode and classic mode) to automatically redirect any unauthenticated page request to the specified login URL. An **authorization** element that denies access to unauthenticated users (denoted by the special symbol "?") is also required to make this redirection work.

Next, you'll find that a-Expense has a Login.aspx page that uses the built-in ASP.NET **Login** control, as shown here.

```
<asp:Login ID="Login1" runat="server"
           OnAuthenticate="Login1OnAuthenticate" ... >
</asp:Login>
```

Finally, if you look at the application, you'll notice that the handler of the Login.aspx page's **OnAuthenticate** event looks like the following.

```csharp
public partial class Login : System.Web.UI.Page
{
    protected void Login1OnAuthenticate(object sender,
                                        AuthenticateEventArgs e)
    {
        var repository = new UserRepository();
        if (!repository.ValidateUser(this.Login1.UserName,
                                        this.Login1.Password))
        {
            e.Authenticated = false;
            return;
        }
        var user = repository.GetUser(this.Login1.UserName);
        if (user != null)
        {
            Session["LoggedUser"] = user;
            e.Authenticated = true;
```

```
        }
    }
}
```

This logic is typical for logon pages. You can see in the code that the user name and password are checked first. Once credentials are validated, the user profile information is retrieved and stored in the session state under the **LoggedUser** key. Notice that the details of interacting with the database have been put inside of the application's **UserRepository** class.

Setting the **Authenticated** property of the **AuthenticatedEventArgs** object to **true** signals successful authentication. ASP.NET then redirects the request back to the original page.

At this point, normal page processing resumes with the execution of the page's **Page_Load** method. In the a-Expense application, this method retrieves the user's profile information that was saved in the session state object and initializes the page's controls. For example, the logic might look like the following.

```
protected void Page_Load(object sender, EventArgs e)
{
    var user = (User)Session["LoggedUser"];
    var repository = new ExpenseRepository();
    var expenses = repository.GetExpenses(user.Id);
    this.MyExpensesGridView.DataSource = expenses;
    this.DataBind();
}
```

The session object contains the information needed to make access control decisions. You can look in the code and see how a-Expense uses an application-defined property called **AuthorizedRoles** to make these decisions.

A-EXPENSE WITH CLAIMS

The developers only had to make a few changes to a-Expense to replace forms authentication with claims. The process of validating credentials was delegated to a claims issuer simply by removing the logon page and by configuring the ASP.NET pipeline to include the Windows Identity Foundation (WIF) **WSFederationAuthentication-Module**. This module detects unauthenticated users and redirects them to the issuer to get tokens with claims. Without a logon page, the application still needs to write profile and authorization data into the session state object, and it does this in the **Session_Start** method. Those two changes did the job.

❖ You only need a few changes to make the application claims aware.

Figure 5 shows how authentication works now that a-Expense is claims-aware.

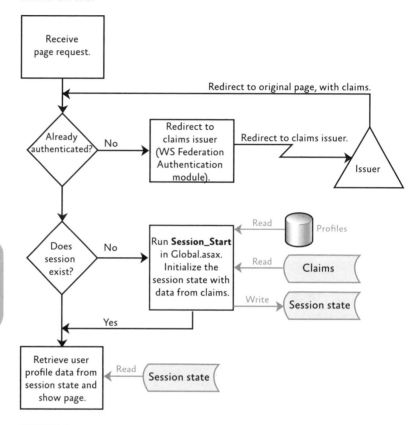

Making a-Expense use claims was easy with WIF's FedUtil. exe utility. See Appendix A.

FIGURE 5
a-Expense with claims processing

The Web.config file of the claims-aware version of a-Expense contains a reference to WIF-provided modules. This Web.config file is automatically modified when you run the FedUtil wizard either through the command line (FedUtil.exe) or through the **Add STS Reference** command by right-clicking the Web project in Visual Studio.

If you look at the modified Web.config file, you'll see that there are changes to the authorization and authentication sections as well as new configuration sections. The configuration sections include the information needed to connect to the issuer. They include, for example, the Uniform Resource Indicator (URI) of the issuer and information about signing certificates.

The first thing you'll notice in the Web.config file is that the authentication mode is set to **None**, while the requirement for authenticated users has been left in place.

We're just giving the highlights here. You'll also want to check out the WIF and ADFS product documentation.

```
<authentication mode="None" />

<authorization>
    <deny users="?" />
</authorization>
```

> **Note:** *The forms authentication module that a-Expense previously used has been deactivated by setting the authentication mode attribute to **None**. Instead, the **WSFederationAuthentication- Module** (FAM) and **SessionAuthenticationModule** (SAM) are now in charge of the authentication process.*

The application's Login.aspx page is no longer needed and can be removed from the application.

Next, you will notice that the Web.config file contains two new modules, as shown here.

```
<httpModules>

    ...

    <add name="WSFederationAuthenticationModule"
        type="Microsoft.IdentityModel.Web.
                    WSFederationAuthenticationModule, ..." />

    <add name="SessionAuthenticationModule"
        type="Microsoft.IdentityModel.Web.
                    SessionAuthenticationModule, ..." />

</httpModules>
```

When the modules are loaded, they're inserted into the ASP.NET processing pipeline in order to redirect the unauthenticated requests to the issuer, handle the reply posted by the issuer, and transform the user token sent by the issuer into a **ClaimsPrincipal** object. The modules also set the value of the **HttpContext.User** property to the **ClaimsPrincipal** object so that the application has access to it.

The **WSFederationAuthenticationModule** redirects the user to the issuer's logon page. It also parses and validates the security token that is posted back. This module writes an encrypted cookie to avoid repeating the logon process. The **SessionAuthenticationModule** detects the logon cookie, decrypts it, and repopulates the **Claims- Principal** object.

The Web.config file contains a new section for the **Microsoft. IdentityModel** that initializes the WIF environment.

```
<configSections>
...
<section name="microsoft.identityModel"
        type="Microsoft.IdentityModel.Configuration.
                            MicrosoftIdentityModelSection,
                    Microsoft.IdentityModel, ..." />
</configSections>
```

The identity model section contains several kinds of information needed by WIF, including the address of the issuer, and the certificates (the **serviceCertificate** and **trustedIssuers** elements) that are needed to communicate with the issuer.

```
<microsoft.identityModel>
  <service>
    <audienceUris>
      <add value=
              "https://{adatum hostname}/ a-expense.claimsAware/"
      />
    </audienceUris>
...
```

> **Note:** *The value of "adatum hostname" changes depending on where you deploy the sample code. In the development environment, it is "localhost."*

Security tokens contain an audience URI. This indicates that the issuer has issued a token for a specific "audience" (application). Applications, in turn, will check that the incoming token was actually issued for them. The **audienceUris** element lists the possible URIs. Restricting the audience URIs prevents malicious clients from reusing a token for a different application that they are not authorized to access.

```
<federatedAuthentication>
  <wsFederation passiveRedirectEnabled="true"
      issuer="https://{adatum host}/{issuer endpoint} "
      realm="https://{adatum host}/a-Expense.ClaimsAware/"
      requireHttps="true" />
  <cookieHandler requireSsl="true" />
</federatedAuthentication>
```

The **federatedAuthentication** section identifies the issuer and the protocol required for communicating with it.

Using HTTPS mitigates man-in-the-middle and replay attacks. This is optional during development, but be sure to use HTTPS in production environments.

```
<serviceCertificate>
   <certificateReference x509FindType="FindBySubjectDistinguishedN
ame"
        findValue="CN=adatum" storeLocation="LocalMachine"
storeName="My" />
</serviceCertificate>
```

The service certificate section gives the location of the certificate used to decrypt the token, in case it was encrypted. Encrypting the token is optional, and it's a decision of the issuer to do it or not. You don't need to encrypt the token if you're using HTTPS, but encryption is generally recommended as a security best practice.

```
<issuerNameRegistry
   type="Microsoft.IdentityModel.Tokens.ConfigurationBasedIssuer-
NameRegistry,
        Microsoft.IdentityModel, ... >
   <trustedIssuers>
      <add thumbprint="0E2A9EB75F1AFC321790407FA4B130E0E4E223E2"
           name="CN=adatum" />
   </trustedIssuers>
</issuerNameRegistry>
```

A thumbprint is the result of hashing an X.509 certificate signature. SHA-1 is a common algorithm for doing that. Thumbprints uniquely identify a certificate and the issuer. The **issuerNameRegistry** element contains the list of thumbprints of the issuers it trusts. Issuers are identified by the thumbprint of their signing X.509 certificate. If the thumbprint does not match the certificate embedded in the incoming token signature, WIF will throw an exception. If the thumbprint matches, the **name** attribute will be mapped to the **Claim.Issuer** property.

In the code example, the name attribute **adatum** is required for the scenario because the a-Expense application stores the federated user name in the roles database. A federated user name has the format: adatum*username*.

The following procedure shows you how to find the thumbprint of a specific certificate.

To find a thumbprint

1. On the taskbar, click **Start**, and then type **mmc** in the search box.

2. Click **mmc**. A window appears that contains the Microsoft Management Console application.

3. On the **File** menu, click **Add/Remove Snap-in**.

4. In the **Add or Remove Snap-ins** dialog box, click **Certificates**, and then click **Add**.

5. In the **Certificates snap-in** dialog box, select **Computer account**, and then click **Next**.

6. In the **Select Computer** dialog box, select **Local computer**, click **Finish**, and then click **OK**.

7. In the left pane, a tree view of all the certificates on your computer appears. If necessary, expand the tree. Expand the Personal folder. Expand the Certificates folder.

8. Click the certificate whose thumbprint you want.

9. In the **Certificate Information** dialog box, click the **Details** tab, and then scroll down until you see the thumbprint.

At this point, you're done. The changes in the Web.config file are enough to delegate authentication to the issuer.

There's still one detail to take care of. Remember from the previous section that the logon handler (which has now been removed from the application) was also responsible for storing the user profile data in the session state object. This bit of logic is relocated to the **Session_Start** method found in the Global.asax file. The **Session_Start** method is automatically invoked by ASP.NET at the beginning of a new session, after authentication occurs. The user's identity is now stored as claims that are accessed from the thread's **CurrentPrincipal** property. Here is what the **Session_Start** method looks like.

This may seem like a lot of configuration, but the FedUtil wizard handles it for you.

```
protected void Session_Start(object sender, EventArgs e)
{
  if (this.Context.User.Identity.IsAuthenticated)
  {
    string issuer =
        ClaimHelper.GetCurrentUserClaim(
            System.IdentityModel.Claims.ClaimTypes.Name).
                                        OriginalIssuer;
    string givenName =
        ClaimHelper.GetCurrentUserClaim(
```

```
            WSIdentityConstants.ClaimTypes.GivenName).Value;

    string surname =
        ClaimHelper.GetCurrentUserClaim(
                WSIdentityConstants.ClaimTypes.Surname).Value;

    string costCenter =
        ClaimHelper.GetCurrentUserClaim(
                        Adatum.ClaimTypes.CostCenter).Value;

    var repository = new UserRepository();
    string federatedUsername =
                GetFederatedUserName(issuer, identity.Name);
    var user = repository.GetUser(federatedUsername);
    user.CostCenter = costCenter;
    user.FullName = givenName + " " + surname;

    this.Context.Session["LoggedUser"] = user;
  }
}
```

Note that the application does not go to the application data store to authenticate the user because authentication has already been performed by the issuer. The WIF modules automatically read the security token sent by the issuer and set the user information in the thread's current principal object. The user's name and some other attributes are now claims that are available in the current security context.

The user profile database is still used by a-Expense to store the application-specific roles that apply to the current user. In fact, a-Expense's access control is unchanged whether or not claims are used.

The preceding code example invokes methods of a helper class named **ClaimHelper**. One of its methods, the **GetCurrentUserClaim** method, queries for claims that apply in the current context. You need to perform several steps to perform this query:

1. Retrieve context information about the current user by getting the static **CurrentPrincipal** property of the **System. Threading.Thread** class. This object has the run-time type **IPrincipal**.

> Putting globally significant data like names and cost centers into claims while keeping app-specific attributes in a local store is a typical practice.

2. Use a run-time type conversion to convert the current principal object from **IPrincipal** to the type **IClaimsPrincipal**. Because a-Expense is now a claims-aware application, the run-time conversion is guaranteed to succeed.

3. Use the **Identities** property of the **IClaimsPrincipal** interface to retrieve a collection of identities that apply to the claims principal object from the previous step. The object that is returned is an instance of the **ClaimsIdentityCollection** class. Note that a claims principal may have more than one identity, although this feature is not used in the a-Expense application.

4. Retrieve the first identity in the collection. To do this, use the collection's indexer property with 0 as the index. The object that is returned from this lookup is the current user's claims-based identity. The object has type **IClaimsIdentity**.

5. Retrieve a claims collection object from the claims identity object with the **Claims** property of the **IClaimsIdentity** interface. The object that is returned is an instance of the **ClaimsCollection** class. It represents the set of claims that apply to the claims identity object from the previous step.

6. At this point, if you iterate through the claims collection, you can select a claim whose claim type matches the one you are looking for. The following expression is an example of how to do this.

```
claims.Single(c => c.ClaimType == claimType)
```

Note that the **Single** method assumes that there is one claim that matches the requested claim type. It will throw an exception if there is more than one claim that matches the desired claim type or if no match is found. The **Single** method returns an instance of the **Claim** class.

7. Finally, you extract the claim's value with the Claim class's **Value** property. Claims values are strings.

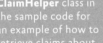
Look at the implementation of the **ClaimHelper** class in the sample code for an example of how to retrieve claims about the current user.

A-ORDER BEFORE CLAIMS

Unlike a-Expense, the a-Order application uses Windows authentication. This has a number of benefits, including simplicity.

Enabling Windows authentication is as easy as setting an attribute value in XML, as shown here.

```
<authentication mode="Windows" />
```

The a-Order application's approach to access control is considerably simpler than what you saw in aExpense. Instead of combining authentication logic and business rules, a-Order simply annotates pages with roles in the Web.config file.

```
<authorization>
   <allow roles="Employee, Order Approver" />
   <deny users="?" />
</authorization>
```

The user interface of the a-Order application varies, depending on the user's current role.

```
base.OnInit(e);

this.OrdersGrid.Visible =
        !this.User.IsInRole("Order approver");

this.OrdersGridForApprovers.Visible =
        this.User.IsInRole("Order approver");
```

A-ORDER WITH CLAIMS

Adding claims to a-Order is really just a configuration step. The application code needs no change.

If you download the project from http://claimsid.codeplex.com, you can compare the Web.config files before and after conversion to claims. It was just a matter of right-clicking the project in Visual Studio and then clicking **Add STS Reference**. The process is very similar to what you saw in the previous sections for the a-Expense application.

The claims types required are still the users and roles that were previously provided by Windows authentication.

```
<claimTypeRequired>
  <claimType type=
    "http://schemas.xmlsoap.org/ws/2005/05/identity/claims/name"
  />
  <claimType type=
    "http://schemas.microsoft.com/ws/2008/06/identity/claims/role"
  />
</claimTypeRequired>
```

◈ *Converting Windows authentication to claims only requires a configuration change.*

Don't forget that more than one value of a given claim type may be present. For example, a single identity can have several role claims.

Signing Out of an Application

The **FederatedPassiveSignInStatus** control is provided by WIF. Here is how the single sign-on scenario uses it to sign out of an application.

```
<idfx:FederatedPassiveSignInStatus
    ID="FederatedPassiveSignInStatus1"
    runat="server"
    OnSignedOut="FederatedPassiveSignInStatus1SignedOut"
    SignOutText="Logout"
    FederatedPassiveSignOut="true"
    SignOutAction="FederatedPassiveSignOut" />
```

The **idfx** prefix identifies the control as belonging to the **Microsoft.IdentityModel.Web.Controls** namespace. The control causes a browser redirect to the ADFS issuer, which logs out the user and destroys any cookies related to the session.

Setup and Physical Deployment

Deploying a claims-aware Web application follows many of the same steps you already know for non–claims-aware applications. The differences have to do with the special considerations of the issuer. Some of these considerations include providing a suitable test environment during development, migrating to a production issuer, and making sure the issuer and the Web application are properly configured for Internet access.

USING A MOCK ISSUER

The downloadable versions of a-Expense and a-Order are set up by default to run on a standalone development workstation. This is similar to the way you might develop your own applications. It's generally easier to start with a single development machine.

To make this work, the developers of a-Expense and a-Order wrote a small stub implementation of an issuer. You can find this code in the downloadable Visual Studio solution. Look for the project with the URL https://localhost/adatum.SimulatedIssuer.

When you first run the a-Expense and a-Order applications, you'll find that they communicate with the stand-in issuer. The issuer issues predetermined claims.

It's not very difficult to write such a component, and you can reuse the sample that's online.

Using a simple, developer-created claims issuer is a good practice during development and unit testing. Your network administrator can help you change the application configuration to use production infrastructure components when it's time for acceptance testing and deployment.

◈ *Mock issuers simplify the development process.*

ISOLATING ACTIVE DIRECTORY

The a-Order application uses Windows authentication. Since developers do not control the identities in their company's enterprise directory, it is sometimes useful to swap out Active Directory with a stub during the development of your application.

The a-Order application (before claims) shows an example of this. To use this technique, you need to make a small change to the Web.config file to disable Windows authentication and then add a hook in the session authentication pipeline to insert the user identities of your choosing. Disable Windows authentication with the following change to the Web.config file.

```
<authentication mode="None" />
```

The Global.asax file should include code that sets the identity with a programmer-supplied identity. The following is an example.

```
<script runat="server">

void Application_AuthenticateRequest(object sender, EventArgs e)
{
  this.Context.User = MaryMay;
}

private static IPrincipal MaryMay
{
  get
  {
    IIdentity identity = new GenericIdentity("mary");
    string[] roles = { "Employee", "Order Approver" };
    return new GenericPrincipal(identity, roles);
  }
}

</script>
```

Remove this code before you deploy your application.

CONVERTING TO A PRODUCTION ISSUER

Remove the mock issuers when you deploy the application.

When you are ready to deploy to a production environment, you'll need to migrate from your simulated issuer that runs on your development workstation to a component such as ADFS 2.0.

Making this change requires two steps. First, you need to modify the Web application's Web.config file using FedUtil so that it points to the production issuer. Next, you need to configure the issuer so that it recognizes requests from your Web application and provides the appropriate claims.

Appendix A of this guide walks you through the process of using FedUtil and shows you how to change the Web.config files.

You can refer to documentation provided by your production issuer for instructions on how to add a relying party and how to add claims rules. Instructions for the samples included in this guide can be found at http://claimsid.codeplex.com.

ENABLING INTERNET ACCESS

One of the benefits of outsourcing authentication to an issuer is that existing applications can be accessed from the external Internet very easily. The protocols for claims-based identity are Internet-friendly. All you need to do is make the application and the issuer externally addressable. You don't need a VPN.

If you decide to deploy outside of the corporate firewall, be aware that you will need certificates from a certificate authority for the hosts that run your Web application and issuer. You also need to make sure that you configure your URLs with fully qualified host names or static IP addresses. The ADFS 2.0 proxy role provides specific support for publishing endpoints on the Internet.

Variation—Moving to Windows Azure

It's easy to move a claims-aware application to Windows Azure.

The last stage of Adatum's plan is to move a-Expense to Windows Azure. Windows Azure uses Microsoft data centers to provide developers with an on-demand compute service and storage to host, scale, and manage Web applications on the Internet. This variation shows the power and flexibility of a claims-based approach. The a-Expense code doesn't change at all. You only need to edit its Web.config file.

Figure 6 shows what Adatum's solution looks like.

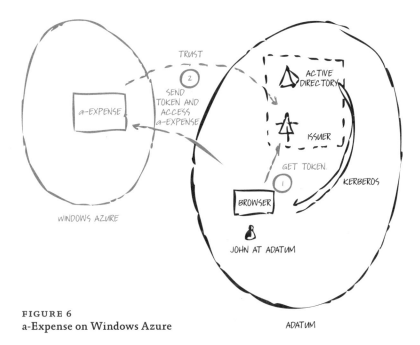

FIGURE 6
a-Expense on Windows Azure

From Adatum's users' viewpoints, the location of the a-Expense application is irrelevant except that the application's URL might change once it is on Azure, but even that can be handled by mapping CNAMEs to Windows Azure URL. Otherwise, its behavior is the same as if it were located on one of Adatum's servers. This means that the sequence of events is exactly the same as before, when a-Expense became claims-aware. The first time a user accesses the application, he will not be authenticated, so the WIF module redirects him to the configured issuer that, in this case, is the Adatum issuer.

The issuer authenticates the user and then issues a token that includes the claims that a-Expense requires, such as the user's name and cost center. The issuer then redirects the user back to the application, where a session is established. Note that, even though it is located on the Internet, aExpense requires the same claims as when it was located on the Adatum intranet.

Obviously, for any user to use an application on Azure, it must be reachable from his computer. This scenario assumes that Adatum's network, including its DNS server, firewalls, and proxies are configured to allow its employees to have access to the Internet.

Notice however, that the issuer doesn't need to be available to external resources. The a-Expense application never communicates with it directly. Instead, it uses browser redirections and follows the protocol for passive clients. For more information about this protocol, see chapter 2, "Claims-Based Architectures" and Appendix B.

Hosting a-Expense on Windows Azure

The following procedures describe how to configure the certificates that you will upload to Windows Azure and the changes you must make to the Web.config file. These procedures assume that you already have a Windows Azure token. If you don't, see http://www.microsoft.com/windowsazure/getstarted/ to learn how to do this.

To configure the certificates

1. In Visual Studio, open the Azure project, such as a-expense.cloud. Right-click the a-Expense.ClaimsAware role, and then click **Properties**.

2. If you need a certificate's thumbprint, click **Certificates**. Along with other information, you will see the thumbprint.

3. Click **Endpoints**, and then select **HTTPS:**. Set the **Name** field to **HttpsIn**. Set the **Port** field to the port number that you want to use. The default is **443**. Select the certificate name from the **SSL certificate name** drop-down box. The default is **localhost**. The name should be the same as the name that is listed on the **Certificates** tab.

Note that the certificate that is uploaded is only used for SSL and not for token encryption. A certificate from Adatum is only necessary if you need to encrypt tokens.

> **Note:** *Both Windows Azure and WIF can decrypt tokens. You must upload the certificate in the Windows Azure portal and configure the Web role to deploy to the certificate store each time there is a new instance. The WIF **<serviceCertificate>** section should point to that deployed certificate.*

The following procedure shows you how to publish the a-Expense application to Windows Azure.

To publish a-Expense to Windows Azure

1. In Microsoft Visual Studio 2008, open the a-expense.cloud solution.

2. Upload the localhost.pfx certificate to the Windows Azure project. The certificate is located at [samples-installation-directory]\Setup\DependencyChecker\certs\localhost.pfx. The password is "xyz".

3. Modify the a-Expense.ClaimsAware application's Web.config file by replacing the **<microsoft.identityModel>** section with the following XML code. You must replace the **{service-url}** element with the service URL that you selected when you created the Windows Azure project.

```
<microsoft.identityModel>
  <service>
    <audienceUris>
      <add value="https://{service-url}.cloudapp.net/" />
    </audienceUris>
    <federatedAuthentication>
      <wsFederation passiveRedirectEnabled="true"
        issuer="https://{adatum host}/{issuer endpoint}/"
        realm="https://{service-url}.cloudapp.net/"
        requireHttps="true" />
        <cookieHandler requireSsl="true" />
    </federatedAuthentication>
    <issuerNameRegistry
      type=
      "Microsoft.IdentityModel.Tokens.
              ConfigurationBasedIssuerNameRegistry,
              Microsoft.IdentityModel, Version=3.5.0.0,
          Culture=neutral,
          PublicKeyToken=31bf3856ad364e35">
      <trustedIssuers>
      <!--Adatum's identity provider -->
        <add thumbprint=
              "f260042d59e14817984c6183fbc6bfc71baf5462"
            name="adatum" />
      </trustedIssuers>
    </issuerNameRegistry>
    <certificateValidation
            certificateValidationMode="None" />
  </service>
</microsoft.identityModel>
```

4. Right-click the a-expense.cloud project, and then click **Publish**. This generates a ServiceConfiguration file and the actual package for Azure.

5. Deploy the ServiceConfiguration file and package to the Windows Azure project.

Once the a-Expense application is deployed to Azure, you can log on to http://windows.azure.com to test it.

> **Note:** *If you were to run this application on more than one role instance in Azure (or in an on-premise Web farm), the default cookie encryption mechanism (which uses DPAPI) is not appropriate, since each machine has a distinct key.*
>
> *In this case, you would need to replace the default **SessionSecurityHandler** object and configure it with a different cookie transformation such as **RsaEncryptionCookieTransform** or a custom one. The "Web farm" sample included in the WIF SDK illustrates this in detail.*

More Information

Appendix A of this guide gives a walkthrough of using FedUtil and also shows you how to edit the Web.config files and where to locate your certificates.

MSDN® contains a number of helpful articles, including *MSDN Magazine*'s "A Better Approach For Building Claims-Based WCF Services" (http://msdn.microsoft.com/en-us/magazine/dd278426.aspx).

To learn more about Windows Azure, see Windows Azure Platform at http://www.microsoft.com/windowsazure/.

4   Federated Identity for Web Applications

Many companies want to share resources with their partners, but how can they do this when each business is a separate security realm with independent directory services, security, and authentication? One answer is federated identity. Federated identity helps overcome some of the problems that arise when two or more separate security realms use a single application. It allows employees to use their local corporate credentials to log on to external networks that have trust relationships with their company. For an overview, see the section "Federating Identity across Realms" in chapter 2, "Claims-Based Architectures."

In this chapter, you'll learn how Adatum lets one of its customers, Litware, use the a-Order application that was introduced in chapter 3, "Claims-Based Single Sign-On for the Web."

Federated identity links independent security realms.

The Premise

Now that Adatum has instituted single sign-on (SSO) for its employees, it's ready to take the next step. Customers also want to use the a-Order program to track an order's progress from beginning to end. They expect the program to behave as if it was an application within their own corporate domain. For example, Litware is a longstanding client of Adatum's. Their sales manager, Rick, wants to be able to log on with his Litware credentials and use the a-Order program to determine the status of all his orders with Adatum. In other words, he wants the same SSO capability that Adatum's employees have. However, he doesn't want separate credentials from Adatum just to use a-Order.

Adatum does not want to maintain accounts for another company's users of its Web application, since maintaining accounts for third-party users can be expensive. Federated identity reduces the cost of account maintenance.

Goals and Requirements

The goal of this scenario is to show how federated identity can make the partnership between Adatum and Litware be more efficient. With federated identity, one security domain accepts an identity that comes from another domain. This lets people in one domain access resources located in the other domain without presenting additional credentials. The Adatum issuer will trust Litware to authoritatively issue claims about its employees.

Other than the goals, this scenario has a few other requirements. One is that Adatum must control access to the order status pages and the information that is displayed, based on the partner that is requesting access to the program. In other words, Litware should only be able to browse through its own orders and not another company's. Furthermore, Litware allows employees like Rick, who are in the Sales department, to track orders.

Another requirement is that, because Litware is only one of Adatum's many partners that will access the program, Adatum must be able to find out which issuer has the user's credentials. This is called *home realm discovery*. For more information, see chapter 2, "Claims-Based Architectures."

One assumption for this chapter is that Litware has already deployed an issuer that uses WS-Federation, just as the Adatum issuer does.

WS-Federation is a specification that defines how companies can share identities across security boundaries that have their own authentication and authorization systems. (For more information about WS-Federation, see chapter 2, "Claims-Based Architectures.") This can only happen when legal agreements between Litware and Adatum that protect both sides are already in place. A second assumption is that Litware should be able to decide which of its employees can access the a-Order application.

Security Assertion Markup Language (SAML) is another protocol you might consider for a scenario like this. ADFS 2.0 supports SAMLP.

Overview of the Solution

◈ *The application can be modified to accept claims from a partner organization.*

Once the solution is in place, when Rick logs on to the Litware network, he will access a-Order just as he would a Litware application. From his perspective, that's all there is to it. He doesn't need a special password or user names. It's business as usual. Figure 1 shows the architecture that makes Rick's experience so painless.

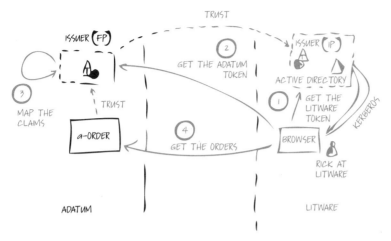

FIGURE 1
Federated identity between Adatum and Litware

As you can see, there have been two changes to the infrastructure since Adatum instituted SSO. A trust relationship now exists between the Adatum and Litware security domains, and the Adatum issuer has been configured with an additional capability: it can now act as a federation provider (FP). A federation provider grants access to a resource, such as the a-Order application, rather than verifying an identity. When processing a client request, the a-Order application relies on the Adatum issuer. The Adatum issuer, in turn, relies on the Litware issuer that, in this scenario, acts as an identity provider (IP). Of course, the diagram represents just one implementation choice; separating Adatum's IP and FP would also be possible. Keep in mind that each step also uses HTTP redirection through the client browser but, for simplicity, this is not shown in the diagram

The following steps grant access to a user in another security domain:

1. Rick is using a computer on Litware's network. He is already authenticated with Active Directory. He opens a browser and navigates to the a-Order application. The application is configured to trust Adatum's issuer (the FP). The application has no knowledge of where the request comes from. It redirects Rick's request to the FP.

2. The FP presents the user with a page listing different identity providers that it trusts. At this point, the FP doesn't know where Rick comes from.

In the sample code, home realm discovery is explicit, but this approach has caveats. For one, it discloses all of Adatum's partners and some companies may not want to do this.

Notice that Adatum's FP is a "relying party" to Litware's IP.

3. Rick selects Litware from the list and then Adatum's FP redirects him to the Litware issuer to verify that Rick is who he says he is.

4. Litware's IP verifies Rick's credentials and returns a security token to Rick's browser. The browser sends the token back to the FP. The claims in this token are configured for the Adatum FP and contain information about Rick that is relevant to Adatum. For example, the claims establish his name and that he belongs to the sales organization. The process of verifying the user's credentials may include additional steps such as presenting a logon page and querying Active Directory or, potentially, other attribute repositories.

5. The Adatum FP validates and reads the security token issued by Litware and creates a new token that can be used by the a-Order application. Claims issued by Litware are transformed into claims that are understood by Adatum's a-Order application. (The mapping rules that translate Litware claims into Adatum claims were determined when Adatum configured its issuer to accept Litware's issuer as an identity provider.)

You can see these steps in more detail in Appendix B. It shows a detailed message sequence diagram for using a browser as the client.

6. As a consequence of the claim mappings, Adatum's issuer removes some claims and adds others that are needed for the a-Order application to accept Rick as a user. The Adatum issuer uses browser redirection to send the new token to the application. WIF validates the security token and extracts the claims. It creates a **ClaimsPrincipal** and assigns it to **HttpContext.User**. The a-Order application can then access the claims for authorization decisions. For example, in this scenario, orders are filtered by organization, which is provided as a claim.

Adatum's issuer, acting as an FP, mediates between the application and the external issuer. You can think of this as a logical role that the Adatum issuer takes on. The FP has two responsibilities. First, it maintains a trust relationship with Litware's issuer, which means that the FP accepts and understands Litware tokens and their claims.

Second, the FP needs to translate Litware claims into claims that a-Order can understand. The a-Order application only accepts claims from Adatum's FP (this is its trusted issuer). In this scenario, a-Order expects claims of type **Role** in order to authorize operations on its Web site. The problem is that Litware claims don't come from Adatum and they don't have roles. In the scenario, Litware claims establish the employee's name and organizational group. Rick's organization, for example, is Sales. To solve this problem, the FP uses mapping rules that turn a Litware claim into an Adatum claim.

The following table summarizes what happens to input claims from Litware after the Adatum FP transforms them into Adatum output claims.

Check out the setup and deployment section of the chapter to see how to establish a trust relationship between issuers in separate trust domains.

Input Conditions	Output claims
Claim issuer: Litware Claim type: Group Claim value: Sales	Claim issuer: Adatum Claim type: Role Claim value: Order Tracker
Claim issuer: Litware	Claims issuer: Adatum Claim type: Company Claim value: Litware
Claim issuer: Litware Claim types name	Claims issuer: Adatum Copy claim

ADFS 2.0 includes a claims rule language that lets you define the behavior of the issuer when it creates new tokens. What all of these rules generally mean is that if a set of conditions is true, you can issue some claims.

These are the three rules that the Adatum FP uses:

- => issue(Type = "http://schemas.adatum.com/claims/2009/08/organization", Value = "Litware");
- c:[Type == "http://schemas.xmlsoap.org/claims/Group", Value == "Sales"] => issue(Type = "http://schemas.microsoft.com/ws/2008/06/identity/claims/role", Issuer = c.Issuer, OriginalIssuer = c.OriginalIssuer, Value = "Order Tracker", ValueType = c.ValueType);
- c:[Type == "http://schemas.xmlsoap.org/ws/2005/05/identity/claims/name"]=> issue(claim = c);

In all the rules, the part before the "=>" is the condition that must be true before the rule applies. The part after the "=>" indicates the action to take. This is usually the creation of an additional claim.

The first rule says that the FP will create a claim of type **Organization** with the value **Litware**. That is, for this issuer (Litware) it will create that claim. The second rule specifies that if there's a claim of type **Group** with value **Sales**, the FP will create a claim of type **Role** with the value **Order Tracker**. The third rule copies a claim of type **name**.

An important part of the solution is home realm discovery. The a-Order application needs to know which issuer to direct users to for authentication. If Rick opens his browser and types **http:// www.adatumpharma.com/ordertracking**, how does a-Order know that Rick can be authenticated by Litware's issuer? The fact is that it doesn't. The a-Order application relies on the FP to make that decision. The a-Order application always redirects users to the FP.

This approach has two potential issues: it discloses information publicly about Litware's relationship with Adatum and it imposes an extra step on users, who might be confused as to which selection is appropriate. It also increases the risk of a phishing attack.

You can resolve these issues by giving the application a hint about the user's home realm. For example, Litware could send a parameter in a query string that specifies the sender's security domain. The application can use this hint to determine the FP's behavior. For more information, see "Home Realm Discovery" in chapter 2, "Claims-Based Architectures."

Benefits and Limitations

Federated identity is an example of how claims support a flexible infrastructure. Adatum can easily add customers by setting up the trust relationship in the FP and by creating the correct claims mappings. Thanks to WIF, dealing with claims in a-Order is straightforward and because Adatum is using ADFS 2.0, creating the claim mapping rules is also fairly simple. Notice that the a-Order application itself didn't change. Also, creating a federation required incremental additions to an infrastructure that was first put in place to implement SSO.

Another benefit is that the claims that Litware issues are about things that make sense within the context of the organization: Litware's employees and their groups. All the identity differences between Litware and Adatum are corrected on the receiving end by Adatum's FP. Litware doesn't need to issue Adatum-specific claims. Although this is technically possible, it can rapidly become difficult and costly to manage as a company adds new relationships and applications.

Federated identity requires a lot less maintenance and troubleshooting. User accounts don't have to be copied and maintained across security realms.

Inside the Implementation

The Visual Studio solution named 2-Federation found at http://claimsid.codeplex.com is an example of how to use federation. The structure of the application is very similar to what you saw in chapter 3, "Claims-Based Single Sign-On for the Web." Adding federated identity did not require recompilation or changes to the Web.config file. Instead, the issuer was configured to act as a federation provider and a trust relationship was established with an issuer that acts as an identity provider. This process is described in the next section. Also, the mock issuers were extended to handle federation provider role.

◈ *Adding federated identity to an existing claims-aware application only requires a configuration change.*

Setup and Physical Deployment

The Visual Studio solution named 2-Federation on CodePlex is initially configured to run on a stand-alone development machine. The solution includes projects that implement mock issuers for both Litware and Adatum.

USING MOCK ISSUERS FOR DEVELOPMENT AND TESTING

Mock issuers are helpful for development, demonstration, and testing because they allow the end-to-end application to run on a single host. The WIF SDK includes a Visual Studio template that makes it easy to create a simple issuer class that derives from the **SecurityToken Service** base class. You then provide definitions for the **GetScope** and

GetOutputClaims methods, as shown in the downloadable code sample that accompanies this scenario.

When the developers at Adatum want to deploy their application, they will modify the configuration so that it uses servers provided by Adatum and Litware. To do this, you need to establish a trust relationship between the Litware and Adatum issuers and modify the a-Order. OrderTracking application's Web.config file for the Adatum issuer.

Establishing Trust Relationships

In the production environment, Adatum and Litware use production-grade security token issuers such as ADFS 2.0. For the scenario to work, you must establish a trust relationship between Adatum's and Litware's issuers. Generally, there are eight steps in this process:

1. You export a public key certificate for token signing from the Litware issuer and copy Litware's token signing certificate to the file system of the Adatum's issuer host.

2. You configure Adatum's issuer to recognize Litware as a trusted identity provider.

3. You configure Litware's issuer to accept requests from the Adatum issuer.

4. You configure a-Order Tracking application as a relying party within the Adatum issuer.

5. You edit claims rules in Litware that are specific to the Adatum issuer.

6. You edit claims transformation rules in the Adatum issuer that are specific to the Litware issuer.

7. You edit claims rules in the Adatum issuer that are specific to the a-Order Tracking application.

You can refer to documentation provided by your production issuer for instructions on how to perform these steps. Instructions for the samples included in this guide can be found at http:// claimsid.codeplex.com.

More Information

For more information about federation and home realm discovery, see "Developer's Introduction to Active Directory Federation Services" at http://msdn.microsoft.com/en-us/magazine/cc163520.aspx. Also see "One does not simply walk into Mordor, or Home Realm Discovery for the Internet" at http://blogs.msdn.com/vbertocci/archive/2009/04/08/one-does-not-simply-walk-into-mordor-or-home-realm-discovery-for-the-internet.aspx.

For a tool that will help you generate WS-Federation metadata documents, see Christian Weyer's blog at http://blogs.thinktecture.com/cweyer/archive/2009/05/22/415362.aspx.

For more information about the ADFS 2.0 claim rule language, see "Claim Rule Language" at http://technet.microsoft.com/en-us/library/dd807118%28WS.10%29.aspx.

5   Federated Identity for Web Services

In chapter 4, "Federated Identity for Web Applications," you saw Adatum make the a-Order application available to its partner Litware. Rick, a salesman from Litware, used his local credentials to log on to the a-Order Web site, which was hosted on Adatum's domain.

To do this, Rick only needed a browser to access the a-Order Web site. But what would happen if the request came from an application other than a Web browser? What if the information supplied by aOrder was going to be integrated into one of Litware's in-house applications?

Federated identity with an active (or "smart") client application works differently than federated identity with a Web browser. In a browser-based scenario, the Web application requests security tokens by redirecting the user's browser to an issuer that produces them. (This process is shown in the earlier scenarios.) With redirection, the browser can handle most of the authentication for you. In the active scenario, the client application actively contacts all issuers in a trust chain (these issuers are typically an IP and an FP) to get and transform the required tokens.

❧ Active clients do not need HTTP redirection.

In this chapter, you'll see an example of a smart client that uses federated identity. Fortunately, support for Windows Communication Foundation (WCF) is a standard feature of the Windows Identity Foundation (WIF). Using WCF and WIF reduces the amount of code needed to implement a claims-aware Web service and a claims-aware smart client.

The Premise

Litware wants to write an application that can read the status of its orders directly from Adatum. To satisfy this request, Adatum agrees to provide a Web service called a-Order.OrderTracking that can be called by Litware over the Internet.

Adatum and Litware have already done the work necessary to establish federated identity, and they both have issuers capable of interacting with active clients. The necessary communications infrastructure, such as firewalls and proxies, is in place. To review these elements, see chapter 4, "Federated Identity for Web Applications."

Now, Adatum only needs to expose a claims-aware Web service on the Internet. Litware will invoke Adatum's Web service from within its client application. Because the client application runs in Litware's security realm, it can use Windows authentication to establish the identity of the user and then use this identity to obtain a token it can pass along to Adatum's FP.

> If ADFS 2.0 is used, support for federated identity with active clients is a standard feature.

Goals and Requirements

Both Litware and Adatum see benefits to a collaboration based on claims-aware Web services. Litware wants programmatic access to Adatum's a-Order application. Adatum does not want to be responsible for authenticating any people or resources that belong to another security realm. For example, Adatum doesn't want to keep and maintain a database of Litware users.

◈ *Active clients use claims to get access to remote services.*

Both Adatum and Litware want to reuse the existing infrastructure as much as possible. For example, Adatum wants to enforce permissions for its Web service with the same rules it has for the browser-based Web application. In other words, the browser-based application and the Web service will both use roles for access control.

Overview of the Solution

Figure 1 gives an overview of the proposed system.

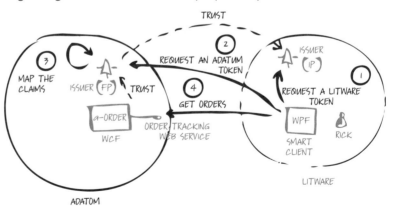

FIGURE 1
Federated identity with a smart client

The diagram shows an overview of the interactions and relationships among the different components. It is similar to the diagrams you saw in the previous chapters, except that no HTTP redirection is involved.

Litware's client application is based on Windows Presentation Foundation (WPF) and is deployed on Litware employees' desktops. Rick, the salesman at Litware, uses this application to track orders with Litware.

Adatum exposes a SOAP Web service on the Internet. This Web service is implemented with WCF and uses standard WCF bindings that allow it to receive Security Assertion Markup Language (SAML) tokens for authentication and authorization. In order to access this service, the client must present a security token from Adatum.

The sequence shown in the diagram proceeds as follows:

1. Litware's WPF application uses Rick's credentials to request a security token from Litware's issuer. Litware's issuer authenticates Rick and, if the authentication is a success, returns a **Group** claim with the value **Sales** because Rick is in the sales organization.

2. The WPF application then forwards the security token to Adatum's issuer, which has been configured to trust Litware's issuer.

3. Adatum's issuer, acting as a federation provider, transforms the claim **Group:Sales** into **Role:Order Tracker** and adds a new claim, **Organization:Litware**. The transformed claims are the ones required by Adatum's Web service, a-Order. OrderTracking. These are the same rules that were defined in the browser-based scenario.

4. Finally, the WPF application sends the Web service the request to return orders. This request includes the security token obtained in the previous step.

This sequence is a bit different from a browser-based Web application because the smart client application knows the requirements of the Web service in advance and also knows how to acquire the claims that satisfy the Web service's requirements. It goes to the IP first, the FP second, and then to the Web service. The smart client application actively drives the authentication process.

Inside the Implementation

◈ *The a-Order.OrderTracking Web service uses WCF standard bindings.*

You can implement a claims-based smart client application using the built-in facilities of WCF or you can code at a lower level using the WIF API. The a-Order.OrderTracking Web service uses WCF standard bindings.

IMPLEMENTING THE WEB SERVICE

The Web service's Web.config file contains the following WCF service configuration.

```xml
<services>
  <service
    name="AOrder.OrderTracking.Services.OrderTrackingService"
    behaviorConfiguration="serviceBehavior">
    <endpoint
      address=""
      binding="ws2007FederationHttpBinding"

      bindingConfiguration=
          "WS2007FederationHttpBinding_IOrderTrackingService"
      contract=
          "AOrder.OrderTracking.Contracts.IOrderTrackingService"
      />
    <endpoint address="mex" binding="mexHttpBinding"
            contract="IMetadataExchange" />
  </service>
</services>
```

> **Note:** *If your service endpoints support metadata exchange, as a-Order tracking does, it's easy for clients to locate services and bind to them using tools such as Svcutil.exe. However, some manual editing of the configuration that is auto-generated by the tools will be necessary in the current example because it involves two issuers: the IP and the FP. With only one issuer, the tool will generate a configuration file that does not need editing.*

The Web.config file contains binding information that matches the binding information for the client. If they don't match, an exception will be thrown.

The Web.config file also contains some customizations. The following XML code shows the first customization.

```
<extensions>
  <behaviorExtensions>
    <add name="federatedServiceHostConfiguration"
         type=
"Microsoft.IdentityModel.
  Configuration.ConfigureServiceHostBehaviorExtensionElement,
 Microsoft.IdentityModel, ..." />
  </behaviorExtensions>
</extensions>
```

Adding this behavior extension attaches WIF to the WCF pipeline. This allows WIF to verify the security token's integrity against the public key. (If you forget to attach WIF, you will see a run-time exception with a message that says that a service certificate is missing.)

The service's Web.config file uses the **<Microsoft.identity Model>** element to specify the configuration required for the WIF component. This is shown in the following code example.

```
<microsoft.identityModel>
  <service>
    <issuerNameRegistry
       type=
         "Microsoft.IdentityModel.Tokens.
             ConfigurationBasedIssuerNameRegistry,
             Microsoft.IdentityModel, Version=3.5.0.0,
           Culture=neutral,
           PublicKeyToken=31bf3856ad364e35">
      <trustedIssuers>
        <add
          thumbprint="f260042d59e14817984c6183fbc6bfc71baf5462"
          name="adatum" />
      </trustedIssuers>
    </issuerNameRegistry>
    <audienceUris>
      <add value=
        "http://{adatum host}/a-Order.OrderTracking.Services/
                              OrderTrackingService.svc"
      />
    </audienceUris>
...
```

Because the Adatum issuer will encrypt its security tokens with the Web service's X.509 certificate, the **<service>** element of the service's Web.config file also contains information about the Web service's private key. This is shown in the following XML code.

```
<serviceCertificate>
   <certificateReference
      findValue="CN=adatum"
      storeLocation="LocalMachine"
      storeName="My"
      x509FindType="FindBySubjectDistinguishedName"/>
</serviceCertificate>
```

IMPLEMENTING THE ACTIVE CLIENT

The client application, which acts as the WCF proxy, is responsible for orchestrating the interactions. You can see this by examining the client's App.config file. The following XML code is in the **<system. serviceModel>** section.

```
<client>
   <endpoint
      address=
        "http://{adatum host}/a-Order.OrderTracking.Services/
                                    OrderTrackingService.svc"
      binding="ws2007FederationHttpBinding"
      bindingConfiguration=
              "WS2007FederationHttpBinding_IOrderTrackingService"
      contract="OrderTrackingService.IOrderTrackingService"
      name="WS2007FederationHttpBinding_IOrderTrackingService">
      <identity>
         <dns value="adatum" />
      </identity>
   </endpoint>
</client>
```

The address attribute gives the Uniform Resource Indicator (URI) of the order tracking service.

The binding attribute, **ws2007FederationHttpBinding**, indicates that WCF should use the WS-Trust protocol when it creates the security context of invocations of the a-Order order tracking service.

The Domain Name System (DNS) value given in the **<identity>** section is verified at run time against the service certificate's subject name.

The App.config file specifies three nested bindings in the **<bindings>** subsection. The following XML code shows the first of these bindings.

```
<ws2007FederationHttpBinding>
  <binding
     name="WS2007FederationHttpBinding_IOrderTrackingService">
    <security mode="Message">
      <message>
        <issuer
          address="https://{adatum host}/{issuer endpoint}"
          binding="customBinding"
          bindingConfiguration="AdatumIssuerIssuedToken">
        </issuer>
      </message>
    </security>
  </binding>
</ws2007FederationHttpBinding>
```

Note: *The issuer address changes depending on how you deploy the sample. For an issuer running on the local machine, the address attribute of the **<issuer>** element will be:*

https://localhost/Adatum.SimulatedIssuer/Scenario4/Issue.svc

For ADFS 2.0, the address will be:

https://{adatum host}/Trust/13/ IssuedTokenMixedSymmetricBasic256

This binding connects the smart client application to the a-Order. OrderTracking service. Unlike WCF bindings that do not involve claims, this special claims-aware binding includes a message security element that specifies the address and binding configuration of the Adatum issuer. The address attribute gives the active endpoint of the Adatum issuer.

◈ *The message security element identifies the issuer.*

The nested binding configuration is labeled **AdatumIssuerIssued-Token**. It is the second binding, as shown here.

```
<customBinding>
  <binding name="AdatumIssuerIssuedToken">
    <security
       authenticationMode="IssuedTokenOverTransport"
       messageSecurityVersion=
          "WSSecurity11WSTrust13WSSecureConversation13
                    WSSecurityPolicy12BasicSecurityProfile10"
    />
       <issuedTokenParameters>
         <issuer
           address=
              "https://{litware host}/Trust/13/UsernameMixed"
```

```
            binding="ws2007HttpBinding"
            bindingConfiguration="LitwareIssuerUsernameMixed">
        </issuer>
      </issuedTokenParameters>
    </security>
    <httpsTransport />
  </binding>
</customBinding>
```

The federation binding in the .NET Framework 3.5 provides no way to turn off a secure conversation. (This feature is available in version 4.0.) Because ADFS 2.0 endpoints have secure conversation disabled, this example needs a custom binding.

Note: *The issuer address changes depending on how you deploy the sample. For an issuer running on the local machine, the address attribute of the* **<issuer>** *element will be:*

https://localhost/Litware.SimulatedIssuer/Scenario4/Issue.svc

For ADFS 2.0 the address will be:

https://{litware host}/Trust/13/UsernameMixed

The **AdatumIssuerIssuedToken** binding configures the connection to the Adatum issuer that will act as the FP in this scenario.

The **<security>** element specifies that the binding uses WS-Trust. This binding also nests the URI of the Litware issuer, and for this reason, it is sometimes known as a *federation binding*. The binding specifies that the binding configuration labeled **LitwareIssuerUsernameMixed** is used for the Litware issuer that acts as the IP. The following XML code shows this.

```
<ws2007HttpBinding>
  <binding name="LitwareIssuerUsernameMixed">
    <security mode="TransportWithMessageCredential">
      <message
        clientCredentialType="UserName"
        establishSecurityContext="false"
      />
    </security>
  </binding>
</ws2007HttpBinding>
```

This binding connects the Litware issuer that acts as an IP. This is a standard WCF HTTP binding because it transmits user credentials to the Litware issuer.

Note: *In a production scenario, the configuration should be changed to **clientCredentialType="Windows"** to use Windows authentication. For simplicity, this sample uses **UserName** credentials. You may want to consider using other options in a production environment.*

When the active client starts, it must provide credentials. If the configured credential type is **UserName**, a **UserName** property must be set. This is shown in the following code.

```
private void ShowOrders()
{
  var client =
          new OrderTrackingService.OrderTrackingServiceClient();

  client.ClientCredentials.UserName.UserName = "LITWARE\\rick";
  client.ClientCredentials.UserName.Password =
                                    "thisPasswordIsNotChecked";

  var orders = client.GetOrdersFromMyOrganization();

  this.DisplayView(new OrderTrackingView()
                  {
                      DataContext =
                          new OrderTrackingViewModel(orders)
                  });
}
```

Using WIF's **WSTrustChannel** gives you more control, but it requires a deeper understanding of WS-Trust.

This step would not be necessary if the application were deployed in a production environment because it would probably use Windows authentication.

> **Note:** *WCF federation bindings can handle the negotiations between the active client and the issuers without additional code. You can achieve the same results with calls to the WIF's **WSTrust-Channel** class.*

IMPLEMENTING THE AUTHORIZATION STRATEGY
The Adatum Web service implements its authorization strategy in the **SimpleClaimsAuthorizationManager** class. The service's Web.config file contains a reference to this class in the **<claimsAuthorization-Manager>** element.

❧ *A claims authorization manager determines which methods can be called by the current user.*

```
<claimsAuthorizationManager
    type="AOrder.OrderTracking.Services.
                        SimpleClaimsAuthorizationManager,
        AOrder.OrderTracking.Services" />
```

Adding this service extension causes WCF to invoke the **Check Access** method of the specified class for authorization. This occurs before the service operation is called.

The implementation of the **SimpleClaimsAuthorizationManager** class is shown in the following code.

```
public class SimpleClaimsAuthorizationManager :
                                    ClaimsAuthorizationManager
{
  public SimpleClaimsAuthorizationManager() { }

  public override bool CheckAccess(AuthorizationContext context)
  {
    return context.Principal.IsInRole(Adatum.Roles.OrderTracker);
  }
}
```

WIF provides the base class, **ClaimsAuthorizationManager**. Applications derive from this class in order to specify their own ways of checking whether an authenticated user should be allowed to call the Web service methods.

The **CheckAccess** method in the a-Order order tracking service ensures that the caller of any of the service's methods must have a role claim with the value **Adatum.Roles.OrderTracker**, which is defined in the **Samples.Web.ClaimsUtilities** project elsewhere as the string "Order Tracker".

In this scenario, the Litware issuer, acting as an IP, issues a **Group** claim that identifies the salesman Rick as being in the Litware sales organization (value=**Sales**). The Adatum issuer, acting as an FP, transforms the security token it receives from Litware. One of its transformation rules adds the role **Order Tracker** to any Litware employee with a group claim value of **Sales**. The order tracking service receives the transformed token and grants access to the service.

DEBUGGING THE APPLICATION

The configuration files for the client and the Web service in this sample include settings to enable tracing and debugging messages. By default, they are commented out so that they are not active.

If you uncomment them, make sure you update the **<shared Listeners>** section so that log files are generated where you can find them and in a location where the application has write permissions. Here is the XML code.

```
<sharedListeners>
  <add
    initializeData="c:\temp\WCF-service.svclog"
    type="System.Diagnostics.XmlWriterTraceListener"
    name="xml">
    <filter type="" />
  </add>
  <add
    initializeData="c:\temp\wcf-service-msvg.svclog"
    type="System.Diagnostics.XmlWriterTraceListener, System,
            Version=2.0.0.0, Culture=neutral,
            PublicKeyToken=b77a5c561934e089"
    name="ServiceModelMessageLoggingListener"
    traceOutputOptions="Timestamp">
    <filter type="" />
  </add>
</sharedListeners>
```

Setup and Physical Deployment

By default, the Web service uses the local host for all components. In a production environment, you would want to use separate computers for the client, the Web service, the FP, and the IP.

To deploy this application, you must substitute the mock issuer with a production-grade component such as ADFS 2.0 that supports active clients. You must also adjust the Web.config and App.config settings to account for the new server names.

❧ *Remove the mock issuer during deployment.*

Note that neither the client nor the Web service needs to be recompiled to be deployed to a production environment. All of the necessary changes are in the respective .config files.

CONFIGURING ADFS 2.0 FOR WEB SERVICES

In the case of ADFS 2.0, you enable the endpoints using the Microsoft Management Console.

To obtain a token from Litware, the **UsernameMixed** or **WindowsMixed** endpoint could be used. **UsernameMixed** requires a user name and password to be sent across the wire, while **WindowsMixed** works with the Windows credentials. Both endpoints will return a SAML token.

Note: *The "Mixed" suffix indicates that the endpoint uses transport security (based on HTTPS) for integrity and confidentiality and message security (based on an X.509 certificate).*

To obtain a token from Adatum, the endpoint used is **IssuedToken-MixedSymmetricBasic256**. This endpoint accepts a SAML token as an input and returns a SAML token as an output. It also uses transport and message security.

In addition, both Litware and Adatum must establish a trust relationship. Litware must configure Adatum ADFS as a relying party and create rules to generate a token based on Lightweight Directory Access Protocol (LDAP) Active Directory attributes. Adatum must configure Litware ADFS as an Identity Provider and create rules to transform the group claims into role claims.

Finally, Adatum must configure the a-Order Web service as a relying party (RP). You must enable token encryption and create rules that pass role and name claims through.

6   Federated Identity with Multiple Partners

In this chapter, you'll learn about the special considerations that apply to applications that establish many trust relationships. Although the basic building blocks of federated identity—issuers, trust, security tokens and claims—are the same as what you saw in the previous chapter, there are some identity and authorization requirements that are particular to the case of multiple trust relationships. This chapter also shows how use the ASP.NET MVC framework to build a claims-aware application.

Special considerations apply when there are many trust relationships.

In some Web applications, such as the one shown in this chapter, users and customers represent distinct concepts. A customer of an application can be an organization, and each customer can have many individual users, such as employees. If the application is meant to scale to large numbers of customers, the enrollment process for new customers must be as streamlined as possible. It may even be automated. As with the other chapters, it is easiest to explain these concepts in the context of a scenario.

The Premise

Fabrikam is a company that provides shipping services. As part of its offering, it has a Web application named Fabrikam Shipping that allows its customers to perform such tasks as creating shipping orders and tracking them. Fabrikam Shipping is an ASP.NET MVC application that runs in Fabrikam's data center. Fabrikam's customers want their employees to use a browser to access the shipping application.

Fabrikam has made its new shipping application claims-based. Like many design choices, this one was customer-driven. In this case, Fabrikam signed a deal with a major customer, Adatum. Adatum's corporate IT strategy (as discussed in chapter 3, "Claims-Based Single Sign-On for the Web") calls for the eventual elimination of identity silos. Adatum wants its users to access Fabrikam Shipping without presenting a separate user names and passwords. Fabrikam also signed agreements with Litware that had similar requirements. However, Fabrikam also wants to support smaller customers, such as Contoso, that do not have the infrastructure in place to support federated identity.

Goals and Requirements

Larger customers such as Adatum and Litware have some particular concerns. These include the following:

- **Usability**. They would prefer if their employees didn't need to learn new passwords and user names for Fabrikam Shipping. These employees shouldn't need any credentials other than the ones they already have, and they shouldn't have to enter credentials a second time when they access Fabrikam Shipping from within their security domain.
- **Support**. It is easier for Adatum and Litware to manage issues such as forgotten passwords than to have employees interact with Fabrikam.
- **Liability**. There are reasons why Adatum and Litware have the authentication and authorization policies that they do. They want to control who has access to resources, no matter where those resources are deployed, and Fabrikam Shipping is no exception. If an employee leaves the company, he or she should no longer have access to the application.

Fabrikam has its own goals, which are the following:

- **To delegate the responsibility for maintaining user identities to its customers, when possible**. This avoids a number of problems, such as having to synchronize data between Fabrikam and its customers. The contact information for a package's sender is an example of this kind of information. Its accuracy should be the customer's responsibility because it could quickly become costly for Fabrikam to keep this information up to date.
- **To bill customers by cost center if one is supplied**. Cost centers should be provided by the customers. This is also another example of information that is the customer's responsibility.
- **To sell its services to a large number of customers**. This means that the process of enrolling a new company must be streamlined. Fabrikam would also prefer that its customers self-manage the application whenever possible.
- **To provide the infrastructure for federation if a customer cannot**. Fabrikam wants to minimize the impact on the application code that might arise from having more than one authentication mechanism for customers.

Overview of the Solution

With the goals and requirements in place, it's time to look at the solution. As you saw in chapter 4, "Federated Identity for Web Applications," the solution includes the establishment of a claim-based architecture with an issuer that acts as an identity provider (IP) on the customers' side. In addition, the solution includes an issuer that acts as the federation provider (FP) on Fabrikam's side. Recall that an FP acts as a gateway between a resource and all of the issuers that provide claims about the resource's users.

Figure 1 shows Fabrikam's solution for customers that have their own IP.

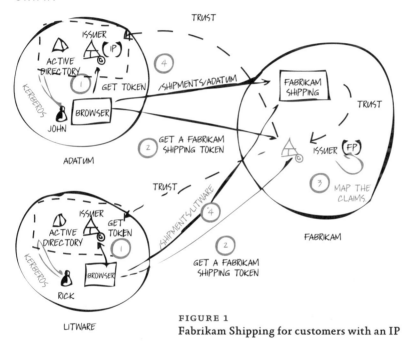

FIGURE 1
Fabrikam Shipping for customers with an IP

Here's an example of how the system works. The steps correspond to the numbers in the preceding illustration.

Step 1: Present Credentials to the IP

1. When John from Adatum attempts to use **Fabrikam Shipping** for the first time (that is, when he first navigates to https://{fabrikam host}/f-shipping/adatum), there's no session established yet. In other words, from Fabrikam's point of views, John is unauthenticated. The URL provides the Fabrikam Shipping application with a hint about the custom-

In this scenario, discovering the home realm is automated. There's no need for the user to provide it, as was shown in chapter 4, "Federated Identity for Web Applications."

er that is requesting access (the hint is "adatum" at the end of the URL).

2. The application redirects John's browser to Fabrikam's issuer (the FP). That is because Fabrikam's FP is the application's trusted issuer. As part of the redirection URL, the application includes the **whr** parameter that provides a hint to the FP about the customer's home realm. The value of the **whr** parameter is http://AdatumADFS/Trust.

3. Fabrikam's FP uses the **whr** parameter to look up the customer's IP and redirect John's browser back to the Adatum issuer.

4. Assuming that John uses a computer that is already a part of the domain and in the corporate network, he will already have valid network credentials that can be presented to Adatum's IP.

5. Adatum's IP uses John's credentials to authenticate him and then issue a security token with a set of Adatum's claims. These claims are the **employee name**, the **employee address**, the **cost center**, and the **department**.

Step 2: Transmit the IP's Security Token to the FP

1. The IP uses HTTP redirection to redirect the security token it has issued to Fabrikam's FP.

2. Fabrikam's FP receives this token and validates it.

Step 3: Map the Claims

1. Fabrikam's FP applies token mapping rules to the IP's security token. The claims are transformed into something that Fabrikam Shipping understands.

2. The FP uses HTTP redirection to submit the claims to John's browser.

Step 4: Transmit the Mapped Claims and Perform the Requested Action

1. The browser sends the FP's security token, which contains the transformed claims, to the Fabrikam Shipping application.

2. The application validates the security token.

3. The application reads the claims and creates a session for John.

Because this is a Web application, all interactions happen through the browser. (See Appendix B for a detailed description of the protocol for a browser-based client.)

The principles behind these interactions are exactly the same as those described in chapter 4, "Federated Identity for Web Applications." One notable exception is Fabrikam's automation of the home realm discovery process. In this case, there's no user intervention necessary. The home realm is entirely derived from information passed first in the URL and then in the **whr** parameter.

Litware follows the same steps as Adatum. The only differences are the URLs used (http://{fabrikam host}/f-shipping/litware and the Litware IP's address) and the claims mapping rules, because the claims issued by Litware are different from those issued by Adatum. Notice that Fabrikam Shipping trusts the Fabrikam FP, not the individual issuers of Litware or Adatum. This level of indirection isolates Fabrikam Shipping from individual differences between Litware and Adatum.

Fabrikam also provides identity services on behalf of customers such as Contoso that do not have issuers of their own. Figure 2 shows how Fabrikam implemented this.

◈ Automated home realm discovery is important when there are many trust relationships.

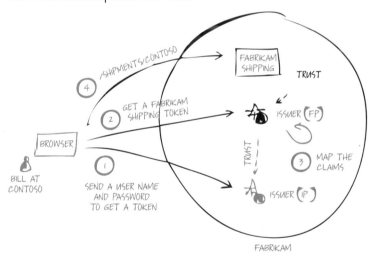

FIGURE 2
Fabrikam Shipping for customers without an IP

Contoso is a small business with no identity infrastructure of its own. It doesn't have an issuer that Fabrikam can trust to authenticate Contoso's users. It also doesn't care if its employees need a separate set of credentials to access the application.

◈ Smaller organizations may not have their own issuers.

Fabrikam has deployed its own IP to support smaller customers such as Contoso. Notice, however, that even though Fabrikam owns this issuer, it's treated as if it were an external IP, just as those that belong to Adatum and Litware. In a sense, Fabrikam "federates with itself."

Because the IP is treated as an external issuer, the process is the same as that used by Adatum and Litware. The only differences are the URLs and the claim mappings.

> **Note:** *By deploying an IP for customers such as Contoso, Fabrikam accepts the costs associated with maintaining accounts for remote users (for example, handling password resets). The benefit is that Fabrikam only has to do this for customers that don't have their own federation infrastructure. Over time, Fabrikam expects to have fewer customers that need this support.*
>
> *It would also be possible for Fabrikam to support third-party identity providers such as LiveID or OpenID as a way to reduce the cost of maintaining passwords for external users.*

USING CLAIMS IN FABRIKAM SHIPPING

◈ *Fabrikam uses claims for access control and for user profiles.*

Fabrikam Shipping uses claims for two purposes. It uses role claims to control access and it also uses claims to retrieve user profile information.

Access control to Fabrikam Shipping is based on one of three roles:

- **Shipment Creator**. Anyone in this role can create new orders.
- **Shipment Manager**. Anyone in this role can create and modify existing shipment orders.
- **Administrator**. Anyone in this role can configure the system. For example, they can set shipping preferences or change the application's appearance and behavior ("look and feel").

The profile information that Fabrikam Shipping expects as claims is the sender's address and the sender's cost center for billing. The cost center allows Fabrikam to provide more detailed invoices. For example, two employees from Adatum who belong to two different departments would get two different bills.

Fabrikam configures claims mappings for every new customer that uses Fabrikam Shipping. This is necessary because the application logic within Fabrikam Shipping only understands one set of role claims, which includes Shipment Creator, Shipment Manager, and Administrator. By providing these mappings, Fabrikam decouples the application from the many different claim types that customers provide.

The following table shows the claims mappings for each customer. Claims that represent cost centers, user names, and sender addresses are simply copied. They are omitted from the table for brevity.

Partner	Input conditions	Output claims
Adatum	Claim issuer: Adatum Claim type: Group Claim value: **Customer Service**	Claim issuer: Fabrikam Claim type: Role Claim value: **Shipment Creator**
	Claim issuer: Adatum Claim type: Group Claim value: **Order Fulfillments**	Claim issuer: Fabrikam Claim type: Group Claim value: **Shipment Creator**
		Claim issuer: Fabrikam Claim type: Group Claim value: **Shipment Manager**
	Claim issuer: Adatum Claim type: Group Claim value: **ItAdmins**	Claim issuer: Fabrikam Claim type: Role Claim value: **Administrator**
	Claim issuer: Adatum	Claim issuer: Fabrikam Claim type: Organization Claim value: **Adatum**
Litware	Claim issuer: Litware Claim type: Group Claim value: **Sales**	Claim issuer: Fabrikam Claim type: Role Claim value: **Shipment Creator**
	Claim issuer: Litware	Claim issuer: Fabrikam Claim type: Organization Claim value: **Litware**
Contoso	Claim issuer: Fabrikam IP Claim type: e-mail Claim value: **bill@contoso.com**	Claim issuer: Fabrikam Claim type: Role Claim value: **Shipment Creator**
		Claim issuer: Fabrikam Claim type: Role Claim value: **Shipment Manager**
		Claim issuer: Fabrikam Claim type: Role Claim value: **Administrator**
		Claim issuer: Fabrikam Claim type: Organization, Claim value: **Contoso**

Note: *As in chapter 4, "Federated Identity for Web Applications," Adatum could issue Fabrikam-specific claims, but it would not be a best practice to clutter Adatum's issuer with Fabrikam-specific concepts such as Fabrikam roles. Fabrikam allows Adatum to issue any claims it wants, and then it configures its FP to map these Adatum claims to Fabrikam claims.*

Inside the Implementation

◈ *Fabrikam Shipping is an ASP.NET MVC application that uses claims.*

The Fabrikam Shipping application uses the ASP.NET MVC framework in conjunction with the Windows Identify Foundation (WIF). The application's Web.config file contains the configuration information, as shown in the following XML code. The **<system.webServer>** section of the Web.config file references WIF-provided modules and the ASP.NET MVC HTTP handler class. The WIF information is same as it was in the previous scenarios. The MVC HTTP handler is in the **<handlers>** section.

```
<system.webServer>
   ...
   <modules runAllManagedModulesForAllRequests="true">
      ...
      <add name="WSFederationAuthenticationModule"
           preCondition=" integratedMode"
           type="Microsoft.IdentityModel.Web.
                         WSFederationAuthenticationModule, ..." />

      <add name="SessionAuthenticationModule"
           preCondition=" integratedMode"
           type="Microsoft.IdentityModel.Web.
                         SessionAuthenticationModule, ..." />
   </modules>
   <handlers>
      ...
      <add name="MvcHttpHandler"
           preCondition="integratedMode"
           verb="*"
           path="*.mvc"
           type="System.Web.Mvc.MvcHttpHandler, ..."/>
      ...
   </handlers>
</system.webServer>
```

Fabrikam chose ASP. NET MVC because it wanted improved testability and a modular architecture. They considered these qualities important for an application with many customers and complex federation relationships.

Note: *Fabrikam Shipping is an example of the finer-grained control that's available with the WIF API. Although Fabrikam Shipping demonstrates how to use MVC with WIF, it's not the only possible approach. Also, WIF-supplied tools, such as FedUtil.exe, are not currently fully integrated with MVC applications. For now, you can edit sections of the configuration files after applying the FedUtil program to an MVC application. This is what the developers at Fabrikam did with Fabrikam Shipping.*

Fabrikam Shipping needs to customize the redirection of HTTP requests to issuers in order to take advantage of the ASP.NET MVC architecture. It does this by turning off automatic redirection from within WIF's federated authentication module. This is shown in the following XML code:

```
<federatedAuthentication>
    <wsFederation passiveRedirectEnabled="false"
      issuer="https://{fabrikam host}/{issuer endpoint}/"
      realm="https://{fabrikam host}/f-Shipping/FederationResult"
      homeRealm="http://tenant-to-be-replaced" requireHttps="true"
    />
    <cookieHandler requireSsl="true" path="/f-Shipping" />
</federatedAuthentication>
```

If you set **passive RedirectEnabled** to **false**, WIF will no longer be responsible for the redirections to your issuers. You will have complete control of these interactions.

By setting the **passiveRedirectEnabled** attribute to **false**, you instruct WIF's federated authentication module not to perform its built-in redirection of unauthenticated sessions to the issuer. For example, Fabrikam Shipping uses the WIF API to perform this redirection under programmatic control.

ASP.NET MVC applications include the concept of *route mappings* and controllers that implement handlers. A route mapping enables you to define URL mapping rules that automatically dispatch incoming URLs to application-provided action methods that process them. (Outgoing URLs are also processed.)

The following code shows how Fabrikam Shipping establishes a routing table for incoming requests such as "http://{fabrikam host}/f-shipping/adatum". The last part of the URL is the name of the organization (that is, the customer). This code is located in Fabrikam Shipping's Global.asax file.

There's a lot of good information about ASP.NET MVC concepts on http://www.asp.net.

```
public class MvcApplication : System.Web.HttpApplication
{
    // ...
    public static void RegisterRoutes(RouteCollection routes)
    {
      // ...
      routes.MapRoute(
          "OrganizationDefault",
          "{organization}/",
          new { controller = "Shipment", action = "Index" });
    }
    // ...
}
```

The **RegisterRoutes** method allows the application to tell the ASP.NET MVC framework how URIs should be mapped and handled in code. This is known as a routing rule.

When an incoming request such as "http://{fabrikam host}/f-Shipping/adatum" is received, the MVC framework evaluates the routing rules to determine the appropriate controller object that should handle the request. The incoming URL is tested against each route rule. The first matching rule is then used to process the request. In the case of the "f-Shipping/adatum" URL, an instance of the application's **ShipmentController** class will be used as the controller, and its **Index** method will be the action method.

```
[AuthenticateAndAuthorize(Roles = "Shipment Creator")]
public class ShipmentController : BaseController
{
    public ActionResult Index()
    {
        // ...
    }
}
```

The **ShipmentController** class has been decorated with a custom attribute named **AuthenticateAndAuthorize**. This attribute is implemented by the Fabrikam Shipping application. Here is the declaration of the attribute class.

```
[AttributeUsage(AttributeTargets.Class | AttributeTargets.
Method)]
public sealed class AuthenticateAndAuthorizeAttribute :
                    FilterAttribute, IAuthorizationFilter
{
  // ...

  public void OnAuthorization(AuthorizationContext filterContext)
  {
    if (!filterContext.HttpContext.Request.IsSecureConnection)
    {
      throw /* ... */
    }

    if (!filterContext.HttpContext.User.Identity.IsAuthenticated)
    {
      AuthenticateUser(filterContext);
    }
    else
    {
      this.AuthorizeUser(filterContext);
    }

  // ...
}
```

The **AuthenticateAndAuthorizeAttribute** class derives from the **FilterAttribute** class and implements the **IAuthorizationFilter** interface. Both these types are provided by ASP.NET MVC. The MVC framework recognizes these attribute types when they are applied to controller classes and calls the **OnAuthorization** method before each controller method is invoked. The **OnAuthorization** method detects whether or not authentication has been performed already, and if it has'nt, it invokes the **AuthenticateUser** helper method to contact the application's federation provider by HTTP redirection. The following code shows how this happens.

To keep your app secure and avoid attacks like SQL injection, you should verify all values from an incoming URL.

```
private static void AuthenticateUser(AuthorizationContext context)
{
    var organizationName =
                (string)context.RouteData.Values["organization"];

    if (!string.IsNullOrEmpty(organizationName))
    {
        if (!IsValidTenant(organizationName)) { throw /* ... */ }

        var returnUrl = GetReturnUrl(context.RequestContext);

        var fam =
            FederatedAuthentication.WSFederationAuthenticationModule;

        var signIn =
            new SignInRequestMessage(new Uri(fam.Issuer), fam.Realm)
            {
                Context = returnUrl.ToString(),
                HomeRealm =RetrieveHomeRealmForTenant(organizationName)
            };

        context.Result =
                new RedirectResult(signIn.WriteQueryString());
    }
}
```

The **AuthenticateUser** method takes the customer's name from the route table. (The code refers to a customer as an organization.) In this example, the customer is "adatum". Next, the method checks to see if the customer has been enrolled in the Fabrikam Shipping application. If not, it raises an exception.

Then, the **AuthenticateUser** method looks up the information it needs to create a federated sign in request. This includes the URI of the issuer (that is, Fabrikam's FP), the application's realm (the address where the issuer will eventually return the security token), the URL that the user is trying to access and the home realm designation of the customer. The method uses this information to create an instance of WIF's **SignInRequestMessage** class. An instance of this class represents a new request to an issuer to authenticate the current user.

In the underlying **WS-Federation** protocol, these pieces of information correspond to the parameters of the request message that will be directed to Fabrikam's FP. The following table shows this correspondence.

Parameter	Name	Contents
wrealm	Realm	This identifies the Fabrikam Shipping application to the FP. This parameter comes from the Web.config file and is the address to which a token should be sent.
wctx	Context	This parameter is set to the address of the original URL requested by the user. This parameter is not used by the issuer, but all issuers in the chain preserve it for the Fabrikam Shipping application, allowing it to send the user to his or her original destination.
whr	Home realm	This parameter tells Fabrikam's FP that it should use Adatum's issuer as the identity provider for this request.

The **GetReturnUrl** method is a locally defined helper method that gives the URL that the user is trying to access. An example is **http://{fabrikam host}/f-shipping/adatum/shipment/new**.

After using the WIF API to construct the sign-on request message, the method configures the result for redirection.

At this point, ASP.NET will redirect the user's browser to the FP. In response, the FP will use the steps described in the chapter 3, "Claims-Based Single Sign-On for the Web," and chapter 4, "Federated Identity for Web Applications," to authenticate the user. This will include additional HTTP redirection to the identity provider specified as the home realm. Unlike the previous examples in this guide, the FP in this example uses the **whr** parameter sent by the application to infer the address of the customer's IP. After the FP receives a security token from the IP and transforms it into a token with the claim types expected by Fabrikam Shipping, it will POST it to the **wrealm** address that was originally specified. This is a special URL configured with the **SignInRequestMessage** class in the **AuthenticateAndAuthorize Attribute** filter. In the example, the URL will be f-shipping/FederationResult.

The MVC routing table is configured to dispatch the POST message to the **FederationResult** action handler defined in the **HomeController** class of the Fabrikam Shipping application. This method is shown in the following code.

```
[ValidateInput(false)]
public ActionResult FederationResult()
{
  var fam =
        FederatedAuthentication.WSFederationAuthenticationModule;
  if (fam.CanReadSignInResponse(
                  System.Web.HttpContext.Current.Request, true))
  {
    string returnUrl = this.GetReturnUrlFromCtx();

    return new RedirectResult(returnUrl);
  }

  // ...
}
```

Notice that this controller does not have the **AuthenticateAnd Authorize** attribute applied. However, the token POSTed to this address is still processed by the WIF Federation Authentication Module because of the explicit redirection of the return URL.

The **FederationResult** action handler uses the helper method **GetReturnUrlFromCtx** to read the **wctx** parameter that contains the original URL requested by the user. This is simply a property lookup operation: **this.HttpContext.Request.Form["wctx"]**. Finally, it issues a redirect request to this URL.

The **ValidateInput** custom attribute is required for this scenario because the body of the POST contains a security token serialized as XML. If this custom attribute were not present, ASP.NET MVC would consider the content of the body unsafe and therefore raise an exception.

The application then processes the request a second time, but in this pass, there is an authenticated user. The **OnAuthorization** method described earlier will again be invoked, except this time it will pass control to the **AuthorizeUser** helper method instead of the **AuthenticateUser** method as it did in the first pass. The definition of the **AuthorizeUser** method is shown in the following code.

```
private void AuthorizeUser(AuthorizationContext context)
{
  var organizationRequested =
    (string)context.RouteData.Values["organization"];
  var userOrganiation =
    ClaimHelper.GetCurrentUserClaim(
        Fabrikam.ClaimTypes.Organization).Value;

  if (!organizationRequested.Equals(userOrganiation,
```

```
                    StringComparison.OrdinalIgnoreCase))
{
    context.Result = new HttpUnauthorizedResult();
    return;
}


var authorizedRoles = this.Roles.Split(new[] { "," },
                        StringSplitOptions.RemoveEmptyEntries);
bool hasValidRole = false;
foreach (var role in authorizedRoles)
{
    if (context.HttpContext.User.IsInRole(role.Trim()))
    {
        hasValidRole = true;
        break;
    }
}

if (!hasValidRole)
{
    context.Result = new HttpUnauthorizedResult();
    return;
}
}
```

The **AuthorizeUser** method checks the claims that are present for the current user. It makes sure that the customer identification in the security token matches the requested customer as given by the URL. It then checks that the current user has one of the roles required to run this application.

> **Note:** *Because this is a claims-aware application, you know that the user object will be of type **IClaimsPrincipal** even though its static type is **IPrincipal**. However, no run-time type conversion is needed in this case. The reason is that the code only checks for role claims, and these operations are available to instances that implement the **IPrincipal** interface.*
>
> *If you want to extract any other claims from the principal, you will need to cast the **User** property to **IClaimsPrincipal** first. This is shown in the following code.*
>
> ```
> var claimsprincipal =
>
>         context.HttpContext.User as IClaimsPrincipal;
> ```

If the user has a claim that corresponds to one of the permitted roles (defined in the **AuthenticateAndAuthorizeAttribute** class), the **AuthorizeUser** method will return without setting a result in the context. This allows the original action request method to run.

In the scenario, the original action method is the **Index** method of the **ShipmentController** class. The method's definition is given by the following code example.

```
[AuthenticateAndAuthorize(Roles = "Shipment Creator")]
public class ShipmentController : BaseController
{
    public ActionResult Index()
    {
      var repository = new ShipmentRepository();

      IEnumerable<Shipment> shipments;
      var organization =
          ClaimHelper.GetCurrentUserClaim(
                          Fabrikam.ClaimTypes.Organization).Value;

      if (this.User.IsInRole(Fabrikam.Roles.ShipmentManager))
      {
        shipments =
              repository.GetShipmentsByOrganization(organization);
      }
      else
      {
        var userName = this.User.Identity.Name;
        shipments =
            repository.GetShipmentsByOrganizationAndUserName(
                                        organization, userName);
      }

      var model =
          new ShipmentListViewModel { Shipments = shipments };

      return View(model);
    }
// ...
}
```

The **Index** action handler retrieves the data is needed to satisfy the request from the application's data store. Its behavior depends on the user's role, which it extracts from the current claims context. It passes control to the controller's **View** method for rendering the information from the repository into HTML.

Setup and Physical Deployment

Applications such as Fabrikam Shipping that use federated identity with multiple partners sometimes rely on automated provisioning and may allow for customer-configurable claims mapping. The Fabrikam Shipping example does not implement automated provisioning, but it includes a prototype of a Web interface as a demonstration of the concepts.

Automated provisioning may be needed when there are many partners.

ESTABLISHING THE TRUST RELATIONSHIP
If you were to implement automated provisioning, you could provide a Web form that allows an administrator from a customer's site to specify a URI of an XML document that contains federation metadata for ADFS 2.0. Alternatively, the administrator could provide the necessary data elements individually.

If your application's FP is an ADFS 2.0 server, you can use Windows PowerShell scripts to automate the configuration steps. For example, the **ADFSRelyingParty** command allows you to programmatically configure ADFS to issue security tokens to particular applications and FPs. Look on MSDN® for the ADFS 2.0 commands that you can use in your PowerShell scripts.

> **Note:** *Processing a federation request might initiate a workflow process that includes manual steps such as verifying that a contract has been signed. Both manual and automated steps are possible, and of course, you would first need to authenticate the request for provisioning.*

If you automate provisioning with a federation metadata XML file, this file would be provided by a customer's issuer. In the following example, you'll see the federation metadata file that is provided by Adatum. The file contains all the information that Fabrikam Shipping would need to configure and deploy its federation provider to communicate with Adatum's issuer. Here are the important sections of the file.

Organization Section

The organization section contains the organization name.

```
<Organization>
  <OrganizationDisplayName xml:lang="">
    Adatum
  </OrganizationDisplayName>
  <OrganizationName xml:lang="">Adatum</OrganizationName>
  <OrganizationURL xml:lang="">
    http://{adatum host}/Adatum.Portal/
  </OrganizationURL>
</Organization>
```

Issuer Section

The issuer section contains the issuer's URI.

```
<fed:SecurityTokenServiceEndpoint>
    <EndpointReference
        xmlns="http://www.w3.org/2005/08/addressing">
        <Address>
            https://{adatum host}/{issuer endpoint}/
        </Address>
    </EndpointReference>
</fed:SecurityTokenServiceEndpoint>
```

Certificate Section

The certificate section contains the certificate (encoded in base64) that is used by the issuer to sign the tokens.

```
<RoleDescriptor ...>
    <KeyDescriptor use="signing">
        <KeyInfo xmlns="http://www.w3.org/2000/09/xmldsig#">
            <X509Data>
                <X509Certificate>
                    MIIB5TCCAV ... Ukyey2pjD/R4LO2B3AO
                </X509Certificate>
            </X509Data>
        </KeyInfo>
    </KeyDescriptor>
</RoleDescriptor>
```

After Adatum registers as a customer of Fabrikam Shipping, the customer's systems administrators must also configure their issuer to respond to requests from Fabrikam's FP. For ADFS 2.0, this process is identical to what you saw in chapter 4, "Federated Identity for Web Applications," when the Litware issuer began to provide claims for the a-Order application.

USER-CONFIGURABLE CLAIMS TRANSFORMATION RULES

It's possible for applications to let customers configure the claims mapping rules that will be used by the application's FP. You would do this to make it as easy as possible for an application's customers to use their existing issuers without asking them to produce new claim types. If a customer already has roles or groups, perhaps from Microsoft® Active Directory®, that are ready to use, it is convenient to reuse them. However, these roles would need to be mapped to roles that are understood by the application.

An application with many partners may require user-configurable claims transformation rules.

If the FP is an ADFS 2.0 server, you can use PowerShell scripts to set up the role mapping rules. The claims mapping rules would be different for each customer.

Appendix A   Using Fedutil

This appendix shows you how to use the FedUtil wizard for the scenarios in this book. Note that a Security Token Service (STS) is equivalent to an issuer.

Using FedUtil to Make an Application Claims-Aware

This procedure shows how to use FedUtil to make an application claims-aware. In this example, the application is a-Order. There are two ways to open the FedUtil tool. One way is to go to the Windows Identity Foundation SDK directory and click **FedUtil.exe**. The other is to open the single sign-on (SSO) solution in Microsoft® Visual Studio®, right-click the a-Order.ClaimsAware project, and then click **Add STS Reference**. In either case, the FedUtil wizard opens.

To make an application claims-aware

1. In the **Application configuration location** box, enter the location of the a-Order Web.config file or browse to it. In the
   Application URI box, enter the Uniform Resource Indicator (URI) for a-Order, and then click **Next**.

2. In the **Security Token Service** dialog box, select **Use an Existing STS**. Alternatively, you can select **Create a new STS project in the current solution** to create a custom STS that you can modify.

3. In the **STS federation metadata location box**, enter the URI of the federation metadata or browse to it, and then click **Next**.

4. In the **Security token encryption** dialog box, select No encryption, and then click **Next**.

5. In the **Offered claims** dialog box, click **Next**.

6. On the Summary page, click Finish.

Along with using FedUtil, you must also make the following changes:

- In the a-Expense Web.config file, change the name of **TrustedIssuer** to **Adatum**. This is necessary because a-Expense uses a custom data store for users and roles mapping. Names should be formatted as Adatum*name*. For example, Adatum\mary is correctly formatted.
- Place the ADFS token signing certificate into the Trusted People store of the local machine.

Appendix B   Message Sequences

Appendix B shows in detail the message sequences for the passive (browser-based) and active (smart) client scenarios. It also includes information about what the HTTP and, where applicable, Kerberos, traffic looks like as the browser or client, application, issuer, and Microsoft® Active Directory® communicate with each other.

The Browser-Based Scenario

Figure 1 shows the message sequence for the browser-based scenario.

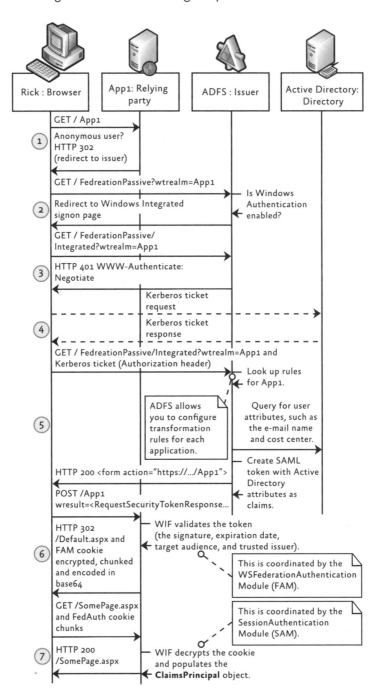

FIGURE 1
Message sequence for the browser-based scenario

Figure 2 shows the traffic generated by the browser.

#	Result	Prot...	Host	URL
1	302	HTTPS	www.adatumpharma.com	/a-Expense.ClaimsAware/
2	302	HTTPS	login.adatumpharma.com	/FederationPassive/?wa=wsignin1.0&wtrealm
3	401	HTTPS	login.adatumpharma.com	/FederationPassive/auth/integrated/Integrat
4	401	HTTPS	login.adatumpharma.com	/FederationPassive/auth/integrated/Integrat
5	200	HTTPS	login.adatumpharma.com	/FederationPassive/auth/integrated/Integrat
6	302	HTTPS	www.adatumpharma.com	/a-Expense.ClaimsAware/
7	200	HTTPS	www.adatumpharma.com	/a-Expense.ClaimsAware/AddExpense.aspx

FIGURE 2
HTTP traffic

The numbers in the screenshot correspond to the steps in the message diagram. In this example, the name of the application is a-Expense.ClaimsAware. For example, step 1 in the screen shot shows the initial HTTP redirect to the issuer that is shown in the message diagram. The following table explains the symbols in the "#" column.

Symbol	Meaning
Arrow	An arrow indicates an HTTP 302 redirect.
Key	A key indicates a Kerberos ticket transaction (the 401 code indicates that authentication is required).
Globe	A globe indicates a response to a successful request, which means that the user can access a Web site.

STEP 1

The anonymous user browses to a-Expense and the **WSFederated-AuthenticationModule** (FAM) redirects the user to the issuer, which, in this example, is located at https://login.adatumpharma.com/FederationPassive. As part of the request URL, there are four query string parameters: **wa** (the action to execute, which is wsignin1.0), **wtrealm** (the relying party that this token applies to, which is a-Expense), **wctx** (this is context data such as a return URL that will be propagated among the different parties), and **wct** (this is a time stamp).

Figure 3 shows the response headers for step 1.

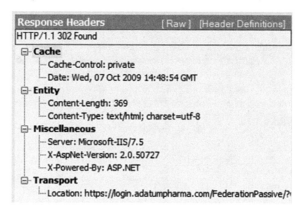

FIGURE 3
Response headers for step 1

The FAM on a-Expense redirects the anonymous user to the issuer.

Figure 4 shows the parameters that are sent to the issuer with the query string.

QueryString	
Name	Value
▶ wa	wsignin1.0
wtrealm	https://www.adatumpharma.com/a-Expense.ClaimsAware/
wctx	rm=0&id=passive&ru=%2fa-Expense.ClaimsAware%2fdefault.aspx
wct	2009-10-07T14:48:55Z

FIGURE 4
Query string parameters

STEP 2

The issuer is Active Directory Federation Services (ADFS) 2.0 configured with Windows Integrated authentication only. Figure 5 shows that ADFS redirects the user to the integrated sign-on page.

> **Note:** *ADFS can be configured to allow Windows Integrated authentication and/or client certificate authentication and/or forms-based authentication. In either case, credentials are mapped to an Active Directory account.*

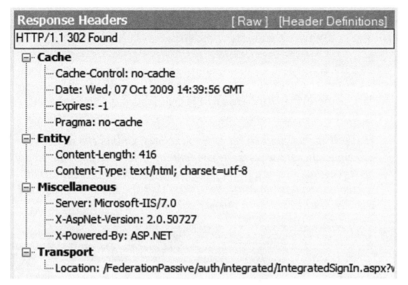

FIGURE 5
ADFS redirecting the user to the Windows Integrated authentication page

STEP 3

The IntegratedSignIn.aspx page is configured to use Windows Integrated authentication on Internet Information Services (IIS). This means that the page will reply with an HTTP 401 status code and the "WWW-Authenticate: Negotiate" HTTP header. This is shown in Figure 6.

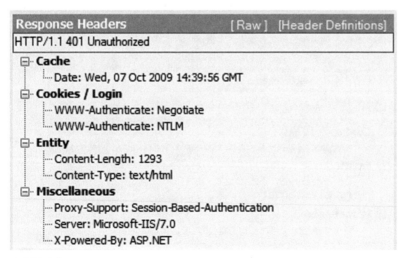

FIGURE 6
ADFS returning WWW-Authenticate: Negotiate header

IIS returns the WWW-Authenticate:Negotiate header to let the browser know that it supports Kerberos or NTLM.

STEP 4
At this point, the user authenticates with Microsoft Windows® credentials, using either Kerberos or NTLM. Figure 7 shows the HTTP traffic for NTLM, not Kerberos.

> **Note**: *If the infrastructure, such as the browser and the service principal names, are correctly configured, the client can avoid step 4 by requesting a service ticket from the key distribution center that is hosted on the domain controller. It can then use this ticket together with the authenticator in the next HTTP request.*

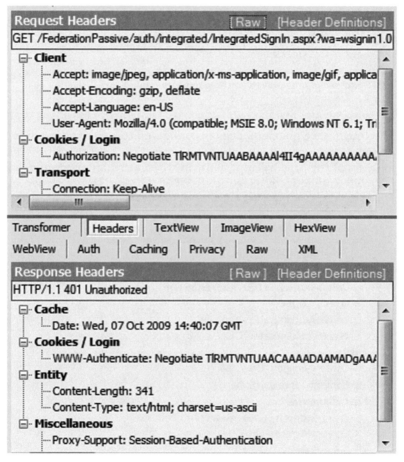

FIGURE 7
NTLM handshake on the ADFS Web site

The Cookies/Login node for the request headers shows the NTLM handshaking process. This process has nothing to do with claims, WS-Federation, SAML, or WS-Trust. The same thing would happen for any site that is configured with Windows Integrated Authentication. Note that this step not occur for Kerberos.

STEP 5
Now that the user has been successfully authenticated with Windows credentials, ADFS can generate a SAML token based on the Windows identity. ADFS looks up the claim mapping rules associated with the application using the **wtrealm** parameter mentioned in step 1 and executes them. The result of those rules is a set of claims that will be included in a SAML assertion and sent to the user's browser.

The following XML code shows the token that was generated (some attributes and namespaces were deleted for clarity).

```
<t:RequestSecurityTokenResponse
  xmlns:t="http://schemas.xmlsoap.org/ws/2005/02/trust">
  <t:Lifetime>
    <wsu:Created>2009-10-22T14:40:07.978Z</wsu:Created>
    <wsu:Expires>2009-10-22T00:40:07.978Z</wsu:Expires>
  </t:Lifetime>
  <wsp:AppliesTo>
    <EndpointReference>
      <Address>
        https://www.adatumpharma.com/a-Expense.ClaimsAware/
      </Address>
    </EndpointReference>
  </wsp:AppliesTo>
  <t:RequestedSecurityToken>
    <saml:Assertion
        MinorVersion="1"
        AssertionID="_9f68..." Issuer="http://.../Trust">
      <saml:Conditions
        NotBefore="2009-10-22T14:40:07.978Z"
        NotOnOrAfter="2009-10-22T00:40:07.978Z">
        <saml:AudienceRestrictionCondition>
          <saml:Audience>
            https://www.adatumpharma.com/a-Expense.ClaimsAware/
          </saml:Audience>
        </saml:AudienceRestrictionCondition>
      </saml:Conditions>
      <saml:AttributeStatement>
        <saml:Subject>
          <saml:SubjectConfirmation>
            <saml:ConfirmationMethod>
```

The **RequestSecurityToken-Response** is defined in the WS-Trust specification. It's the shell that will enclose a token of any kind. The most common implementation of the token is SAML (version 1.1 or 2.0). The shell contains the lifetime and the endpoint address for this token.

The token expiration date (for WS-Fed).

The token audience (for WS-Fed).

The SAML token is represented by an assertion that contains certain conditions such as the expiration time and audience restrictions.

The token audience (for SAML).

```
                urn:oasis:names:tc:SAML:1.0:cm:bearer
            </saml:ConfirmationMethod>
          </saml:SubjectConfirmation>
        </saml:Subject>
        <saml:Attribute
            AttributeName="name"
            AttributeNamespace=
                "http://.../ws/2005/05/identity/claims">
            <saml:AttributeValue>mary</saml:AttributeValue>
        </saml:Attribute>
        <saml:Attribute
            AttributeName="CostCenter"
            AttributeNamespace=
                "http://schemas.adatumpharma.com/2009/08/claims">
            <saml:AttributeValue>394002</saml:AttributeValue>
        </saml:Attribute>
      </saml:AttributeStatement>
      <ds:Signature>
        <ds:SignedInfo>
        ...
        </ds:SignedInfo>
        <ds:SignatureValue>
            dCHtoNUbvVyz8...n0XEA6BI=

        <KeyInfo>
          <X509Data>
            <X509Certificate>
                MIIB6DCC...gUitvS6JhHdg
            </X509Certificate>
          </X509Data>
        </KeyInfo>
      </ds:Signature>
    </saml:Assertion>
  </t:RequestedSecurityToken>
  <t:TokenType>
      http://docs.oasis-open.org/wss/
          oasis-wss-saml-token-profile-1.1#SAMLV1.1
  </t:TokenType>
  <t:RequestType>
      http://schemas.xmlsoap.org/ws/2005/02/trust/Issue
  </t:RequestType>
  <t:KeyType>
      http://schemas.xmlsoap.org/ws/2005/05/identity/NoProofKey
  </t:KeyType>
</t:RequestSecurityTokenResponse>
```

*Because the browser does not hold a key that can prove its identity, the token generated is of type **bearer**. In this scenario, enabling HTTPS is critical to avoid potential attacks.*

*The claims are represented by the SAML attributes, where **ClaimType** equals the **AttributeNamespace** and the **AttributeName**. The **ClaimValue** equals the **AttributeValue**.*

The signature and the public key (an X.509 certificate that is encoded in base64) that will be used to verify the signature on the Web site. If the verification was successful you have to ensure that the certificate is the one you trust (either by checking its thumbprint or its serial number).

The token generated is SAM 1.1.

STEP 6

Once ADFS generates a token, it needs to send it back to the application. A standard HTTP redirect can't be used because the token may be 4 KB long, which is larger than most browsers' size limit for an URL. Instead, issuers generate a **<form>** that includes a POST method. The token is in a hidden field. A script auto-submits the form once the page loads. The following HTML code shows the issuer's response.

```html
<html>
  <head>
    <title>Working...</title>
  </head>
  <body>
    <form
      method="POST"
      name="hiddenform"
      action=
        "https://www.adatumpharma.com/a-Expense.ClaimsAware/">
      <input type="hidden" name="wa" value="wsignin1.0" />
      <input
        type="hidden"
        name="wresult"
        value="&lt;t:RequestSecurityTokenResponse
                xmlns...&lt;/t:RequestSecurityTokenResponse>"
      />
      <input
        type="hidden"
        name="wctx"
        value="rm=0&amp;id=passive&amp;
                ru=%2fa-Expense.ClaimsAware%2fdefault.aspx"
      />
      <noscript>
        <p>Script is disabled. Click Submit to continue.</p>
        <input type="submit" value="Submit" />
      </noscript>
    </form>
    <script language="javascript">
      window.setTimeout('document.forms[0].submit()', 0);
    </script>
  </body>
</html>
```

When the application receives the POST, the FAM takes control of the process. It listens for the **AuthenticateRequest** event. Figure 8 shows the sequence of steps that occur on the handler of the **AuthenticateRequest** event.

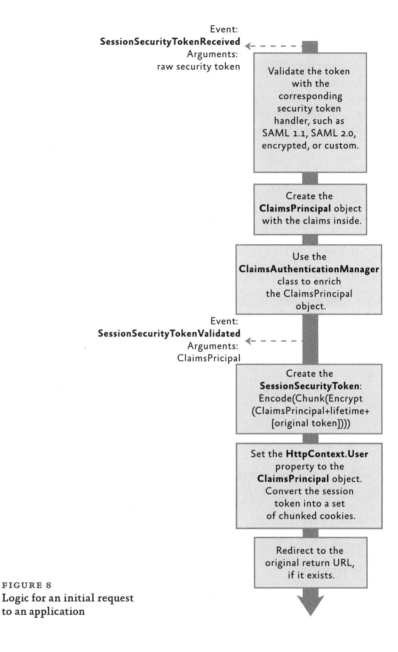

Event:
SessionSecurityTokenReceived
Arguments:
raw security token

Validate the token
with the
corresponding
security token
handler, such as
SAML 1.1, SAML 2.0,
encrypted, or custom.

Create the
ClaimsPrincipal object
with the claims inside.

Use the
ClaimsAuthenticationManager
class to enrich
the ClaimsPrincipal
object.

Event:
SessionSecurityTokenValidated
Arguments:
ClaimsPricipal

Create the
SessionSecurityToken:
Encode(Chunk(Encrypt
(ClaimsPrincipal+lifetime+
[original token])))

Set the **HttpContext.User**
property to the
ClaimsPrincipal object.
Convert the session
token into a set
of chunked cookies.

Redirect to the
original return URL,
if it exists.

FIGURE 8
Logic for an initial request
to an application

Notice that one of the steps that the FAM performs is to create the session security token. In terms of network traffic, this token is a set of cookies named **FedAuth[n]** that is the result of compressing, encrypting, and encoding the **ClaimsPrincipal** object. The cookies are chunked to avoid exceeding any cookie size limitations. Figure 9 shows the HTTP response, where a session token is chunked into three cookies.

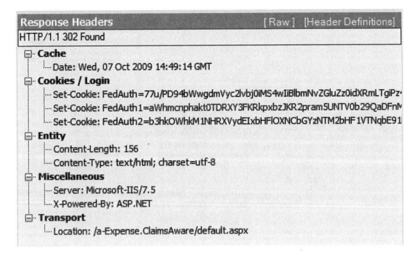

FIGURE 9
HTTP response from the Web site with a session token chunked into three cookies

STEP 7

The session security token (the FedAuth cookies) is sent on subsequent requests to the application. In the same way that the FAM handles the **AuthenticationRequest** event, the SAM executes the logic shown in Figure 10.

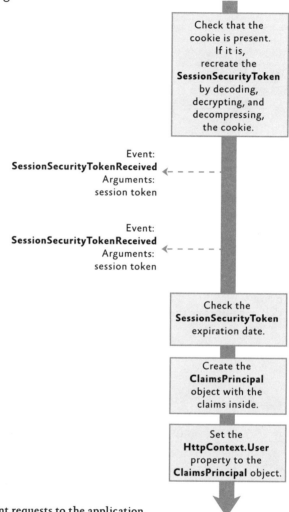

Event:
SessionSecurityTokenReceived
Arguments:
session token

Event:
SessionSecurityTokenReceived
Arguments:
session token

FIGURE 10
Logic for subsequent requests to the application

The **FedAuth** cookies are sent on each request. Figure 11 shows the network traffic.

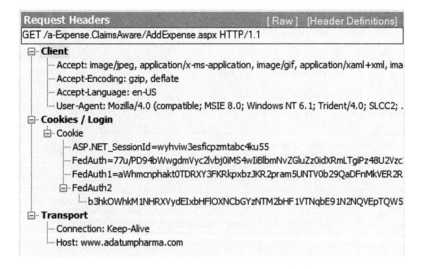

FIGURE 11
Traffic for a second HTTP request

The Active Client Scenario

The following section shows the interactions between an active client and a Web service that is configured to trust tokens generated by an ADFS issuer. Figure 12 shows a detailed message sequence diagram.

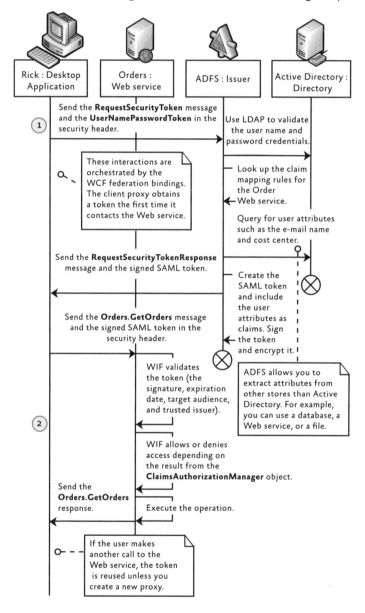

FIGURE 12
Active client scenario message-diagram

Figure 13 shows the corresponding HTTP traffic for the active client message sequence.

Action	From/To
http://docs.oasis-open.org/ws-sx/ws-trust/200512/RST/Issue	https://login.adatumpharma.com/adfs/services/trust/13/usernamemixed
http://docs.oasis-open.org/ws-sx/ws-trust/200512/RSTRC/IssueFinal	
http://tempuri.org/GetOrders	http://orders.adatumpharma.com/Orders.svc
http://tempuri.org/GetOrdersResponse	

FIGURE 13
HTTP traffic

These are the two steps, explained in detail.

STEP 1

The Orders Web service is configured with the **wsFederationHttp-Binding**. This binding specifies a Web service policy that requires the client to add a SAML token to the SOAP security header in order to successfully invoke the Web service. This means that the client must first contact the issuer with a set of credentials (the user name and password) to get the SAML token. The following message represents a **RequestSecurityToken** (RST) sent to the ADFS issuer (ADFS) hosted at https://login.adatumpharma.com/adfs/services/trust/13/usernamemixed. (Note that the XML code is abridged for clarity. Some of the namespaces and elements have been omitted.)

```
<s:Envelope>
  <s:Header>
    <a:Action>
      http://docs.oasis-open.org/ws-sx/ws-trust/200512/RST/Issue
    </a:Action>
    <a:To>
      https://login.adatumpharma.com/adfs/
                          services/trust/13/usernamemixed
    </a:To>
    <o:Security>
      <o:UsernameToken
        u:Id="uuid-bffe89aa-e6fa-404d-9365-d078d73beca5-1">
        <o:Username>
          <!-- Removed-->
        </o:Username>
        <o:Password>
          <!-- Removed-->
        </o:Password>
      </o:UsernameToken>
    </o:Security>
```

This is the endpoint of the issuer that accepts a **UsernameToken**.

These are the credentials that are sent to the issuer.

```
      </s:Header>
      <s:Body>
        <trust:RequestSecurityToken
          xmlns:trust=
                  "http://docs.oasis-open.org/ws-sx/ws-trust/200512">
          <wsp:AppliesTo>
            <EndpointReference>
              <Address>
                  https://orders.adatumpharma.com/Orders.svc
              </Address>
            </EndpointReference>
          </wsp:AppliesTo>
          <trust:TokenType>
            http://docs.oasis-open.org/wss/
                oasis-wss-saml-token-profile-1.1#SAMLV1.1
          </trust:TokenType>
          <trust:KeyType>
            http://docs.oasis-open.org/ws-sx/
                                    ws-trust/200512/SymmetricKey
        </trust:KeyType>
        </trust:RequestSecurityToken>
      </s:Body>
</s:Envelope>
```

> *The client specifies the intended recipient of the token. In this case, it is the Orders Web service.*

> *The issuer expects a SAML 1.1 token.*

The issuer uses the credentials to authenticate the user and executes the corresponding rules to obtain user attributes from Active Directory (or any other attributes store it is configured to contact).

```
<s:Envelope>
  <s:Header>

<a:Action>http://docs.oasis-open.org/ws-sx/ws-trust/200512/RSTRC/
IssueFinal</a:Action>
  </s:Header>
  <s:Body>
    <trust:RequestSecurityTokenResponseCollection
xmlns:trust="http://docs.oasis-open.org/ws-sx/ws-trust/200512">
      <trust:RequestSecurityTokenResponse>
        <trust:Lifetime>
          <wsu:Created>2009-10-22T21:15:19.010Z</wsu:Created>
          <wsu:Expires>2009-10-22T22:15:19.010Z</wsu:Expires>
        </trust:Lifetime>
        <wsp:AppliesTo>
          <a:EndpointReference>
            <a:Address>
                https://orders.adatumpharma.com/Orders.svc
```

> *The issuer specifies the lifetime of the token.*

> *The issuer specifies the intended recipient of the token. In this case, it is the Orders Web service.*

```
      </a:Address>
    </a:EndpointReference>
  </wsp:AppliesTo>
  <trust:RequestedSecurityToken>
    <xenc:EncryptedData>
      <xenc:EncryptionMethod
        Algorithm=
          "http://www.w3.org/2001/04/xmlenc#aes256-cbc" />
      <KeyInfo>
        <e:EncryptedKey>
          <KeyInfo>
            <o:SecurityTokenReference>
              <X509Data>
                <X509IssuerSerial>
                  <X509IssuerName>
                    CN=localhost
                  </X509IssuerName>
                  <X509SerialNumber>
                    -124594669148411034902102654305925584353
                  </X509SerialNumber>
                </X509IssuerSerial>
              </X509Data>
            </o:SecurityTokenReference>
          </KeyInfo>
          <e:CipherData>
            <e:CipherValue>
              WayfmLM9DA5....u17QC+MWdZVCA2ikXwBc=
            </e:CipherValue>
          </e:CipherData>
        </e:EncryptedKey>
      </KeyInfo>
      <xenc:CipherData>
        <xenc:CipherValue>
          U6TLBMVR/M4Ia2Su....../oV+qg/VU=
        </xenc:CipherValue>
      </xenc:CipherData>
    </xenc:EncryptedData>
  </trust:RequestedSecurityToken>
  <trust:RequestedProofToken>
    <trust:ComputedKey>
      http://docs.oasis-open.org/ws-sx/
                              ws-trust/200512/CK/PSHA1
    </trust:ComputedKey>
  </trust:RequestedProofToken>
  <trust:TokenType>
```

> The token was encrypted using an X.509 certificate (public key). The Web service must have the corresponding private key to decrypt it. This section acts as a hint to help the Web service select the correct key.

> This is the encrypted token. The token is a SAML assertion that represents claims about the user. It's signed with the issuer's private signing key (see below for the decrypted SAML assertion).

```
        http://docs.oasis-open.org/wss/
            oasis-wss-saml-token-profile-1.1#SAMLV1.1
      </trust:TokenType>
      <trust:KeyType>
        http://docs.oasis-open.org/ws-sx/
                          ws-trust/200512/SymmetricKey
      </trust:KeyType>
    </trust:RequestSecurityTokenResponse>
  </trust:RequestSecurityTokenResponseCollection>
</s:Body>
</s:Envelope>
```

> The token that is generated is a SAML 1.1 token.

If you had the private key to decrypt the token (highlighted above as "<e:CipherValue>U6TLBMVR/M4Ia2Su...”), the following is what you would see.

```
<saml:Assertion
  MajorVersion="1"
  MinorVersion="1"
  AssertionID="_a5c22af0-b7b2-4dbf-ac10-326845a1c6df"
  Issuer="http://login.adatumpharma.com/Trust"
  IssueInstant="2009-10-22T21:15:19.010Z ">
  <saml:Conditions
      NotBefore="2009-10-22T21:15:19.010Z "
      NotOnOrAfter="2009-10-22T22:15:19.010Z ">
      <saml:AudienceRestrictionCondition>
        <saml:Audience>
          https://orders.adatumpharma.com/Orders.svc
        </saml:Audience>
      </saml:AudienceRestrictionCondition>
  </saml:Conditions>
  <saml:AttributeStatement>
    <saml:Subject>
      <saml:SubjectConfirmation>
        <saml:ConfirmationMethod>
          urn:..:SAML:1.0:cm:holder-of-key
        </saml:ConfirmationMethod>
        <KeyInfo>
          <trust:BinarySecret>
            ztGzs3I...VW+6Th38o=
          </trust:BinarySecret>
        </KeyInfo>
      </saml:SubjectConfirmation>
    </saml:Subject>
    <saml:Attribute
```

> This is the issuer identifier (it's a URI). It is different than the actual issuer sign-on URL.

> The holder-of-key provides proof of ownership of a signed SAML token. SOAP clients often use this approach to prove that an incoming request is valid. Note that a browser can't access a key store the way a smart client can.

```
     AttributeName="name"
     AttributeNamespace=
         "http://schemas.xmlsoap.org/ws/2005/05/identity/claims">
     <saml:AttributeValue>rick</saml:AttributeValue>
   </saml:Attribute>
   <saml:Attribute
     AttributeName="role"
     AttributeNamespace=
       "http://schemas.xmlsoap.org/ws/2005/05/identity/claims">

     <saml:AttributeValue>OrderTracker</saml:AttributeValue>
   </saml:Attribute>
 </saml:AttributeStatement>
 <ds:Signature>
   <ds:SignedInfo> ... </ds:SignedInfo>
     <ds:SignatureValue>
         dCHtoNUbvVyz8...n0XEA6BI=
     </ds:SignatureValue>
     <KeyInfo>
       <X509Data>
         <X509Certificate>
           MIIB6DCC...gUitvS6JhHdg
         </X509Certificate>
       </X509Data>
     </KeyInfo>
   </ds:Signature>
</saml:Assertion>
```

*The claims are represented by the SAML attributes. The **ClaimType** equals the **AttributeNamespace** and the **AttributeName**. The **ClaimValue** equals the **AttributeValue**.*

This is the signature and public key (an X.509 certificate encoded in base64) that will be used to verify the signature on the Web service. If the verification is successful you must ensure that the certificate is the one you trust, either checking its thumbprint or its serial number.

STEP 2

Once the client obtains a token from the issuer, it can attach the token to the SOAP security header and call the Web service. This is the SOAP message that is sent to the Orders Web service.

```
<s:Envelope>
  <s:Header>

    <a:Action>http://tempuri.org/GetOrders</a:Action>
    <a:To>https://orders.adatumpharma.com/Orders.svc</a:To>
    <o:Security>
      <u:Timestamp u:Id="_0">
        <u:Created>2009-10-22T21:15:19.123Z</u:Created>
        <u:Expires>2009-10-22T21:20:19.123Z</u:Expires>
      </u:Timestamp>
      <xenc:EncryptedData >
```

These are the SOAP action and the URL of the Web service.

```
    ... the token we've got in step 1 ...
  </xenc:EncryptedData>
  <Signature xmlns="http://www.w3.org/2000/09/xmldsig#">
    ...
    <SignatureValue>
      oaZFLr+1y/I2kYcAvyQv6WSkPYk=
    </SignatureValue>
    <KeyInfo>
      <o:SecurityTokenReference>
        <o:KeyIdentifier
          ValueType=
            "http://docs.oasis-open.org/wss/
              oasis-wss-saml-token-profile-1.0#
              SAMLAssertionID">
          _a5c22af0-b7b2-4dbf-ac10-326845a1c6df
        </o:KeyIdentifier>
      </o:SecurityTokenReference>
    </KeyInfo>
  </Signature>
  </o:Security>
</s:Header>
<s:Body>
  <GetOrders xmlns="http://tempuri.org/">
    <customerId>1231</customerId>
  </GetOrders>
</s:Body>
</s:Envelope>
```

This is the token from step 1, but encrypted.

This is the signature of the message generated using the SAML Assertion. This is a different signature from the token signature. This signature is generated for any security token (not just a SAML token) to protect the message content and source verification.

Windows Identity Foundation (WIF) and Windows Communication Foundation (WCF) will take care of decrypting and validating the SAML token. The claims will be added to the **ClaimsPrincipal** object and the principal will be added to the WCF security context. The WCF security context will be used in the authorization manager by checking the incoming claims against the operation call the client wants to make.

Appendix C   Industry Standards

This appendix lists the industry standards that are discussed in this book.

Security Assertion Markup Language (SAML)

For more information about SAML, see the following:
- The OASIS Standard specification, "Assertions and Protocol for the OASIS Security Assertion Markup Language (SAML) V1.1"
  http://www.oasis-open.org/committees/download. php/3406/oasis-sstc-saml-core-1.1.pdf

(Chapter 1, "An Introduction to Claims," and chapter 2, "Claims-Based Architectures," cover SAML assertions.)

WS-Federation

For more information about WS-Federation, see the following:
- The OASIS Standard specification, http://docs.oasis-open.org/wsfed/federation/v1.2/
- "Understanding WS-Federation" on MSDN® http://msdn.microsoft.com/en-us/library/bb498017.aspx

WS-Federation: Passive Requestor Profile

For more information about WS-Federation Passive Requestor Profile, see the following:
- Section 13 of the OASIS Standard specification, "Web Services Federation Language (WS-Federation) Version 1.2" **http://docs.oasis-open.org/wsfed/federation/v1.2/os/ ws-federation-1.2-spec-os.html#_Toc223175002**

- "WS-Federation: Passive Requestor Profile" on MSDN
  http://msdn.microsoft.com/en-us/library/bb608217.aspx

WS-Security

For more information about WS-Security, see the following:
- The OASIS Standard specification, "Web Services Security:
  SOAP Message Security 1.1 (WS-Security 2004)"
  **http://docs.oasis-open.org/wss/v1.1/wss-v1.1-spec-os-
  SOAPMessageSecurity.pdf**

WS-SecureConversation

For more information about WS-SecureConversation, see the following:
- The OASIS Standard specification, "WS-SecureConversation
  1.3"
  **http://docs.oasis-open.org/ws-sx/ws-secureconversation/
  v1.3/ws-secureconversation.pdf**

WS-Trust

For more information about WS-Trust, see the following:
- The OASIS Standard specification, "WS-Trust 1.3"
  **http://docs.oasis-open.org/ws-sx/ws-trust/200512/
  ws-trust-1.3-os.html**

XML Encryption

For more information about XML Encryption (used to generate XML
digital signatures), see the following:
- The W3C Recommendation, "XML Encryption Syntax and
  Processing"
  http://www.w3.org/TR/2002/REC-xmlenc-core-20021210/

Appendix D — Certificates

This appendix lists the digital certificates that are used in claims-based applications. To see this in table form, see "Claims Based Identity & Access Control Guide" on CodePlex (http://claimsid.codeplex.com).

Certificates for Browser-Based Applications

In browser-based scenarios, you will find certificates used on the issuer and on the computer that hosts the Web application. The client computer does not store certificates.

ON THE ISSUER (BROWSER SCENARIO)

In browser-based scenarios, you will find the following certificates on the issuer.

Certificate for TLS/SSL (Issuer, Browser Scenario)

The Transport Layer Security (TLS) protocol, Secure Sockets Layer (SSL) protocol uses a certificate to protect the communication with the issuer—for example, for the credentials transmitted to it. The purpose is to avoid man-in-the-middle attacks, eavesdropping, and replay attacks.

Requirements: The subject name in the certificate must match the Domain Name System (DNS) name of the host that provides the certificate. Browsers will generally check that the certificate has a chain of trust to one of the root authorities trusted by the browser.

Recommended certificate store: LocalMachine\My

Example: CN=login.adatumpharma.com

Certificate for Token Signing (Issuer, Browser Scenario)

The issuer's certificate for token signing is used to generate an XML digital signature to ensure token integrity and source verification.

Requirements: The worker process account that runs the issuer needs access to the private key of the certificate.

Recommended certificate store: LocalMachine\My and if ADFS 2.0 is the issuer, the ADFS 2.0 database will keep a copy.

Example: CN=adatumpharma-tokensign.com

> **Note**: *The subject name on the certificate does not need to match a DNS name. It's a recommended practice to name the certificate in a way that describes its purpose.*

Optional Certificate for Token Encryption (Issuer, Browser Scenario)

The certificate for token encryption secures the SAML token. Encrypting tokens is optional, but it is recommended. For example, you may opt to rely on TLS/SSL that will secure the whole channel.

Requirements: Only the public key is required. The private key is owned by the relying party to decrypt.

Recommended certificate store: LocalMachine\TrustedPeople, LocalMachine\AddressBook or if ADFS 2.0 is the issuer, the ADFS 2.0 database will keep it.

Example: CN=a-expense.adatumpharma-tokenencrypt.com

> **Note:** *Encrypting the token is optional, but it is generally recommended. Using TLS/SSL is already a measure to ensure confidentiality of the token in transit. This is an extra security measure that could be used in cases where claim values are confidential.*

ON THE WEB APPLICATION SERVER

In browser-based scenarios, you will find the following certificates on the Web application server.

Certificate for TLS/SSL (Web Server, Browser Scenario)

The Transport Layer Security (TLS) Secure Sockets Layer (SSL) protocol uses a certificate to protect the communication with the Web application server—for example, for the SAML token posted to it. The purpose is to avoid man-in-the-middle attacks, eavesdropping, and replay attacks.

Requirements: The subject name in the certificate must match the DNS name of the host that provides the certificate. Browsers will generally check that the certificate has a chain of trust to one of the root authorities trusted by the browser.

Recommended certificate store: LocalMachine\My

Example: CN=a-expense.adatumpharma.com

Token Signature Verification (Web Server, Browser Scenario)

The Web application server has the thumbprint of the certificate that is used to verify the SAML token signature. Issuer embeds the certificate in each digitally signed security token. The Web application server checks that the digital signature's thumbprint (a hash code) matches that of the signing certificate. WIF and ADFS embed the public key in the token by default.

Requirements: The thumbprint of the issuer's certificate should be present in the **<issuerNameRegistry>** section of the application's Web.config file.

Recommended certificate store: None.

Example: d2316a731b59683e744109278c80e2614503b17e (This is the thumbprint of the certificate with CN=adatumpharma-tokensign. com.)

> **Note:** *If the certificate (Issuer public key) is embedded in the token, the signature verification is done automatically by WIF. If not, an **IssuerTokenResolver** needs to be configured to find the public key. This is common in interop scenarios; however, WIF and ADFS will always embed the full public key.*

Token Signature Chain Trust Verification (Web Server, Browser Scenario)

The Web application server has a certificate that is used to ensure a trusted certificate chain for the issuer token signing certificate.

Requirements: The public key of the issuer certificate should be installed in LocalMachine\TrustedPeople or the certificate was issued by a trusted root authority.

Recommended certificate store: LocalMachine\TrustedPeople only if the certificate was not issued by a trusted root authority.

> **Note:** *The chain trust verification is controlled by an attribute of the **<certificateValidation>** element of WIF configuration section of the application's Web.config file. WIF has this setting turned on by default.*

Optional Token Decryption
(Web Server, Browser Scenario)

The Web application has a certificate that it uses to decrypt the SAML token that it receives from an issuer (if it was encrypted). The Web application has both public and private keys. The issuer has only the public key.

Requirements: The certificate used to decrypt should be configured in the **<serviceCertificate>** element of the **<microsoft.identity Model>** section of the application's Web.config. Also, the App Pool account of the Web site should have permission to read the private key of the certificate.

Recommended certificate store: LocalMachine\My

Example: CN=a-expense.adatumpharma-tokenencrypt.com

Cookie Encryption/Decryption
(Web Server, Browser Scenario)

The Web application server has a certificate that it uses to ensure confidentiality of the session cookie created to "cache" the token claims for the whole user session.

Requirements: The default WIF mechanism uses DPAPI to encrypt the cookie. This requires access to a private key stored in the profile of the App Pool account. You must ensure that the account has the profile loaded by setting the Load User Profile to true in the App Pool configuration.

Recommended certificate store: None

> **Note:** *A more Web-farm friendly option is using a different* **CookieTransform** *to encrypt/decrypt the token (like* **RsaEncryptionCookieTransform***) that uses X.509 certificates instead of DPAPI.*

Certificates for Active Clients

In scenarios with active clients that interact with Web services, you will find certificates used on the issuer, on the machine that hosts the Web service and on the client machine.

ON THE ISSUER (ACTIVE SCENARIO)

In active client scenarios, you will find the following certificates on the issuer.

Certificate for Transport Security (TLS/SSL) (Issuer, Active Scenario)

The Transport Layer Security (TLS) Secure Sockets Layer (SSL) protocol uses a certificate to protect the communication with the issuer—for example, for the credentials transmitted to it. The purpose is to avoid man-in-the-middle attacks, eavesdropping, and replay attacks.

Requirements: The subject name in the certificate must match the DNS name of the host that provides the certificate. Browsers will generally check that the certificate has a chain of trust to one of the root authorities trusted by the browser.

Recommended certificate store: LocalMachine\My

Example: CN=login.adatumpharma.com

Certificate for Message Security (Issuer, Active Scenario)

A certificate will be used to protect the communication between the client and the issuer at the message level.

Requirements: For a custom issuer that you implement, the service credentials are configured in the WCF Issuer—for example, through **<serviceCertificate>** section of the issuer's Web.config file.

For an ADFS 2.0 issuer, this is configured using the MMC console.

Recommended certificate store: LocalMachine\My or ADFS database

Example: CN=login.adatumpharma.com

Certificate for Token Signing (Issuer, Active Scenario)

The issuer's certificate for token signing is used to generate an XML digital signature to ensure token integrity and source verification.

Requirements: The worker process account that runs the issuer needs access to the private key of the certificate.

Recommended certificate store: LocalMachine\My and the ADFS v2 database

Example: CN=adatumpharma-tokensign.com

> **Note**: *The subject name on the certificate does not need to match a DNS name. It's a recommended practice to name the certificate in a way that describes it purpose.*

Certificate for Token Encryption
(Issuer, Active Scenario)

The certificate for token encryption secures the SAML token. This certificate is required when an active client is used.

Requirements: Only the public key is required. The private key is owned by the relying party to decrypt.

Recommended certificate store: LocalMachine\TrustedPeople, Local-Machine\AddressBook or the ADFS 2.0 database.

Example: CN=a-expense.adatumpharma-tokenencrypt.com

> **Note:** *Encrypting the token is optional, but it is generally recommended. Using TLS/SSL is already a measure to ensure confidentiality of the token in transit. This is an extra security measure that could be used in cases where claim values are confidential.*

ON THE WEB SERVICE HOST

These are the certificates used on the machine that hosts the Web service.

Certificate for Transport Security
(TLS/SSL) (Web Service Host, Active Scenario)

The Transport Layer Security (TLS) Secure Sockets Layer (SSL) protocol uses a certificate to protect the communication with the Web service—for example, for the SAML token sent to it by an issuer. The purpose is to mitigate and prevent man-in-the-middle attacks, eavesdropping, and replay attacks.

Requirements: The subject name in the certificate must match the DNS name of the host that provides the certificate. Active clients will generally check that the certificate has a chain of trust to one of the root authorities trusted by that client.

Recommended certificate store: LocalMachine\My

Example: CN=a-expense-svc.adatumpharma.com

Certificate for Message Security
(Web Service Host, Active Scenario)

A certificate will be used to protect the communication between the client and the Web service at the message level.

Requirements: The service credentials are configured in the WCF Web service—for example, through **<serviceCertificate>** section of the Web service's Web.config file.

Recommended certificate store: LocalMachine\My

Example: CN=a-expense-svc.adatumpharma.com

Token Signature Verification
(Web Service Host, Active Scenario)

The Web services host has the thumbprint of the certificate that is used to verify the SAML token signature. The issuer embeds the certificate in each digitally signed security token. The Web server host server checks that the digital signature's thumbprint (a hash code) matches that of the signing certificate. WIF and ADFS embed the public key in the token by default.

Requirements: The thumbprint of the issuer's certificate should be present in the **<issuerNameRegistry>** section of the Web service's Web.config file.

Recommended certificate store: None.

Example: d2316a731b59683e744109278c80e2614503b17e (This is the thumbprint of the certificate with CN=adatumpharma-tokensign. com.)

> **Note:** *If the certificate (Issuer public key) is embedded in the token, the signature verification is done automatically by WIF. If not, an* ***IssuerTokenResolver*** *needs to be configured to find the public key. This is common in interop scenarios; however, WIF and ADFS will always embed the full public key.*

Token Decryption (Web Service Host, Active Scenario)

The Web server host has a certificate that it uses to decrypt the SAML token that it receives from an issuer. The Web application has both public and private keys. The issuer has only the public key.

Requirements: The certificate used to decrypt should be configured in the **<serviceCertificate>** element of the **<microsoft.identityModel>** section of the Web service's Web.config file. Also, the App Pool account of the Web server should have permission to read the private key of the certificate.

Recommended certificate store: LocalMachine\My

Example: CN=a-expense-svc.adatumpharma-tokenencrypt.com

Token Signature Chain Trust Verification
(Web Service Host, Active Scenario)

The Web service host has a certificate that is used to ensure a trusted certificate chain for the issuer token signing certificate.

Requirements: The public key of the issuer certificate should be installed in LocalMachine\TrustedPeople or the certificate was issued by a trusted root authority.

Recommended certificate store: LocalMachine\TrustedPeople only if the certificate was not issued by a trusted root authority.

> **Note:** *The chain trust verification is controlled by an attribute of the* **<certificateValidation>** *element of WIF configuration section of the Web service's Web.config file. WIF has this setting turned on by default.*

ON THE ACTIVE CLIENT HOST
These are the certificates that are used on the active client computer.

Certificate for Message Security (Active Client Host)
A certificate will be used to protect the communication between the client and the Web service or issuer at the message level.

Requirements: If **negotiateServiceCredentials** is enabled, the client will obtain the public key of the Web service or issuer at run time. If not, certificate for message security is configured in the WCF client by setting **ClientCredentials.ServiceCertificate** property at run time or configuring the **<serviceCertificate>** element of the active client's App.config file. The service credentials are configured in the WCF Web service—for example, through the **<serviceCertificate>** section of the Web service's Web.config file.

Recommended certificate store: LocalMachine\TrustedPeople or LocalMachine\AddressBook

Example: CN=a-expense-svc.adatumpharma.com

Glossary

access control. The process of making authorization decisions for a given resource.

access control rule. A statement that is used to transform one set of claims into another set of claims. For example, a statement that subjects that possess claim "Role=Contributor" should also have claim "CanAddDocuments=True" as an example of an access control rule. Each access control system will have its own rule syntax and method for applying rules to input claims.

access control system (ACS). The aspect of a software system responsible for authorization decisions.

account management. The process of maintaining user identities.

ActAs. A delegation role that allows a third party to perform operations on behalf of a subject via impersonation.

active client. A claims-based application component that makes calls directly to the claims provider. Compare with passive client.

Active Directory Federation Services (ADFS). An issuer that is a component of the Windows® operating system. It issues and transforms claims, enables federations, and manages user access.

active federation. A technique for accessing a claims provider that does not involve the redirection feature of the HTTP protocol. With active federation, both endpoints of a message exchange are claims-aware. Compare with passive federation.

assertion. Within a closed domain models of security, a statement about a user that is inherently trusted. Assertions, with inherent trust, may be contrasted with claims, which are only trusted to the extent that a trust relationship exists with the issuer of the claim.

authentication. The process of verifying an identity.

authority. The trusted possessor of a private key.

authorization. See *authorization decision*.

authorization decision. The determination of whether a subject with a given identity can gain access to a given resource.

back-end server. A computing resource that is not exposed to the Internet or that does not interact directly with the user.

blind credential. A trusted fact about a user that does not reveal the identity of the user but is relevant for making an authorization decision. For example, an assertion that the user is over the age of 21 may be used to grant access.

bootstrap token. A security token that is passed to a claims provider as part of a request for identity delegation. This is part of the ActAs delegation scenario.

certificate. A digitally signed statement of identity.

certificate authority. An entity that issues X.509 certificates.

claim. A statement about a subject; for example, a name, identity, key, group, permission, or capability made by one subject about itself or another subject. Claims are given one or more values and then packaged in security tokens that are distributed by the issuer.

claims model. The vocabulary of claims chosen for a given application. The claims provider and claims-based application must agree on this vocabulary of claims. When developing a claims-based application, you should code to the claims model instead of calling directly into platform-specific security APIs.

claims processing. A software feature that enables a system to act as a claims provider, claims requester, or claims-based application. For example, a security token service provides claims processing as part of its feature set.

claims producer. A claims provider.

claims provider. A software component or service that generates security tokens upon request. Also known as the issuer of a claim.

claims requester. The client of a security token service. An identity selector is a kind of claims requester.

claims transformer. A claims provider that accepts security tokens as input; for example, as a way to implement federated identity or access control.

claims type. A string, typically a URI, that identifies the kind of claim. All claims have a claims type and a value. Example claims types include **FirstName**, **Role**, and the **PPID** (this stands for private personal identifier). The claims type provides context for the claim value.

claims value. The value of the statement in the claim being made. For example, if the claims type is **FirstName**, a value might be Matt.

claims-based application. A software application that uses claims as the basis of identity and access control. This is in contrast to applications that directly invoke platform-specific security APIs.

claims-based identity. A set of claims from a trusted issuer that denote user characteristics such as the user's legal name or e-mail address. In an application that uses the Windows Identity Foundation, claims-based identity is represented by run-time objects with the **IClaimsIdentity** interface.

claims-based identity model. A way to write applications so that the establishment of user identity is external to the application itself. The environment provides all required user information in a secure manner.

client. An application component that invokes Web services or issues HTTP requests on behalf of a local user.

cloud. A dynamically scalable environment such as Windows Azure for hosting Internet applications.

cloud application. A software system that is designed to run in the cloud.

cloud provider. An application hosting service.

cloud service. A Web service that is exposed by a cloud application.

credentials. Data elements used to establish identity or permission, often consisting of a user name and password.

credential provisioning. The process of establishing user identities, such as user names and initial passwords, for an application.

cryptography. Mathematical algorithms that make reading data dependent on knowledge of a key string.

digital signature. The output of a cryptographic algorithm that provides evidence that the message's originator is authentic and that the message content has not been modified in transit.

domain. Area of control. Domains are often hierarchically structured.

domain controller. A centralized issuer of security tokens for an enterprise directory.

enterprise directory. A centralized database of user accounts for a domain. For example, the Microsoft Active Directory® Domain Service allows organizations to maintain an enterprise directory.

enterprise identity backbone. The chosen mechanism for providing identity and access control within an organization; for example, by running ADFS.

federated identity. A mechanism for authenticating a system's users based on trust relationships that distribute the responsibility for authentication to a claims provider that is outside of the current security realm.

federatedAuthentication attribute. An XML attribute used in a Web.config file to indicate that the application being configured is a claims-based application.

federation provider. A federation provider is a type of identity provider that provides single sign-on functionality between an organization and other identity providers (issuers) and relying parties (applications).

federation provider security token service (FP-STS). A software component or service that is used by a federation provider to accept tokens from a federation partner and then generate claims and security tokens on the contents of the incoming security token into a format consumable by the relying party (application). A security token service that receives security tokens from a trusted federation partner or IP-STS. In turn, the RP-STS issues new security tokens to be consumed by a local relying party application.

FedUtil. The FedUtil.exe utility provided by the Windows Identity Foundation for the purpose of establishing federation.

forest. A collection of domains governed by a central authority. Active Directory Federation Services (ADFS) can be used to combine two Active Directory forests in a single domain of trust.

forward chaining logic. An algorithm used by access control systems that determines permissions based on the application of transitive rules such as group membership or roles. For example, using forward chaining logic an access control system can deduce that user X has permission Z whenever user X has role Y and role Y implies permission Z.

home realm discovery. The process of determining a user's issuer.

identity. Claims-based identity. There are other meanings of the word "identity," so we will further qualify the term when an alternate meaning is intended.

identity delegation. Enabling a third party to act on one's behalf.

identity model. The organizing principles used to establish the identity of an application's user. See *claims-based identity model*.

identity provider (IP). An organization issuing claims in security tokens. For example, a credit card provider organization might issue a claim in a security token that enables payment if the application requires that information to complete an authorized transaction.

identity security token service (I-STS). An identity provider.

information card. A visual representation of an identity with associated metadata that may be selected by a user in response to an authentication request.

input claims. The claims given to a claims transformer such as an access control system.

issuer. The claims provider for a security token, that is, the entity that possesses the private key used to sign a given security token. In the **IClaimsIdentity** interface, the **Issuer** property returns the claims provider of the associated security token. The term may be used more generally to mean the issuing authority of a Kerberos ticket or X.509 certificate, but this second use is always made clear in the text.

issuer name registry. A list of URIs of trusted issuers. You can implement a class derived from the abstract class **IssuerNameRegistry** (this is part of the Windows Identity Foundation) in order to pick an issuer naming scheme and also implement custom issuer validation logic.

issuing authority. Claims provider, the issuer of a security token. (The term has other meanings that will always be made clear with further qualification in the text.)

Kerberos. The protocol used by Active Directory domain controllers to allow authentication in a networked environment.

Kerberos ticket. An authenticating token used by systems that implement the Kerberos protocol, such as domain controllers.

key. A data element, typically a number or a string, that is used by a cryptographic algorithm when encrypting plain text or decrypting cipher text.

key distribution center (KDC). In the Kerberos protocol, a key distribution center is the issuer of security tickets.

Lightweight Directory Access Protocol (LDAP). A TCP/IP protocol for querying directory services in order to find other e-mail users on the Internet or corporate intranet.

Local Security Authority (LSA). A component of the Windows operating system that applications can use to authenticate and log users on to the local system.

Local Security Authority Subsystem Service (LSASS). A component of the Windows operation system that enforces security policy.

managed information card. An information card provided by an external identity provider. By using managed cards, identity information is stored with an identity provider, unlike a self-issued card.

management APIs. Programmable interface for configuration or maintenance of a data set. Compare with portal.

moniker. An alias used consistently by a user in multiple sessions of an application. A user with a moniker often remains anonymous.

multiple forests. A domain model that is not hierarchically structured.

multi-tenant architecture. A cloud-based application designed for running in multiple data centers, usually for the purpose of geographical distribution or fault tolerance.

on-premises computing. Software systems that run on hardware and network infrastructure owned and managed by the same enterprise that owns the system being run.

output claims. The claims produced by a claims transformer such as an output control system.

passive client. A Web browser that interacts with a claims-based application running on an HTTP server.

passive federation. A technique for accessing claims provider that involves the redirection feature of the HTTP protocol. Compare with active federation.

perimeter network. A network that acts as a buffer between an internal corporate network and the Internet.

permission. The positive outcome of an authorization decision. Permissions are sometimes encoded as claims.

personalization. A variant of access control that causes the application's logic to change in the presence of particular claims. Security trimming is a kind of personalization.

policy. A statement of addresses, bindings, and contracts structured in accordance with the WS-Policy specification. It includes a list of claim types that the claims-based application needs in order to execute.

portal. Web interface that allows viewing and/or modifying data stored in a back-end server.

principal. A run-time object that represents a subject. Claims-based applications that use the Windows Identity Foundation expose principals using the **IClaimsPrincipal** interface.

private key. In public key cryptography, the key that is not published. Possession of the correct private key is considered to be sufficient proof of identity.

privilege. A permission to do something such as access an application or a resource.

proof key. A cryptographic token that prevents security tokens from being used by anyone other than the original subject.

public key. In public key cryptography, the key that is published. Possession of a user's public key allows the recipient of a message sent by the user to validate the message's digital signature against the contents of the message. It also allows a sender to encrypt a message so that only the possessor of the private key can decrypt the message.

public key cryptography. A class of cryptographic algorithms that use one key to encrypt data and another key to decrypt this data.

public key infrastructure (PKI). Conventions for applying public key cryptography.

realm. A security realm.

relying party (RP). An application that relies on security tokens and claims issued by an identity provider.

relying party security token service (RP-STS). See *federation provider security token service*.

resource. A capability of a software system or an element of data contained by that system; an entity such as a file, application, or service that is accessed via a computer network.

resource security token service (R-STS). A claims transformer.

REST protocols. Data formats and message patterns for representational state transfer (REST), which abstracts a distributed architecture into resources named by URIs connected by interfaces that do not maintain connection state.

role. An element of identity that may justify the granting of permission. For example, a claim that "role is administrator" might imply access to all resources. The concept of role is often used by access control systems based on the RBAC model as a convenient way of grouping users with similar access needs.

role-based access control (RBAC). An established authorization model based on users, roles, and permissions.

SAML 2.0. A data format used for encoding security tokens that contain claims. Also, a protocol that uses claims in SAML format. See *Security Assertion Markup Language (SAML)*.

scope. In Microsoft Access Control Services, a container of access control rules for a given application.

Security Assertion Markup Language (SAML). A data format used for encoding security tokens that contain claims. Also, a particular protocol that uses claims in SAML format.

security attribute. A fact that is known about a user because it resides in the enterprise directory (thus, it is implicitly trusted). Note that with claims-based identity, claims are used instead of security attributes.

security context. A .NET Framework concept that corresponds to the **IPrincipal** interface. Every .NET Framework application runs in a particular security context.

security infrastructure. A general term for the hardware and software combination that implements authentication, authorization, and privacy.

security policy. Rules that determine whether a claims provider will issue security tokens.

security token. An on-the-wire representation of claims that has been cryptographically signed by the issuer of the claims, providing strong proof to any relying party as to the integrity of the claims and the identity of the issuer.

security token service (STS). A claims provider implemented as a Web service that issues security tokens. ADFS is an example of a security token service. Also known as an issuer. A Web service that issues claims and packages them in encrypted security tokens (see *WS-Security* and *WS-Trust*).

security trimming. (informal) The process of altering an application's behavior based on a subject's available permissions.

service. A Web service that adheres to the SOAP standard.

service provider. A service provider is an application. The term is commonly used with the Security Assertion Markup Language (SAML).

session key. A private cryptographic key shared by both ends of a communications channel for the duration of the communications session. The session key is negotiated at the beginning of the communication session.

SOAP. A Web standard that governs the format of messages used by Web services.

software as a service (SaaS). A software licensing method in which users license software on demand for limited periods of time rather than purchasing a license for perpetual use. The software vendor often provides the execution environment as, for example, a cloud-based application running as a Web service.

subject. A person. In some cases, business organizations or software components are considered to be subjects. Subjects are represented as principals in a software system. All claims implicitly speak of a particular subject. The Windows Identity Foundation type **IClaimsPrincipal** represents the subject of a claim.

System.IdentityModel.dll. A component of the .NET Framework 3.0 that includes some claims-based features, such as the **Claim** and **ClaimSet** classes.

token. A data element or message.

trust. The acceptance of another party as being authoritative over some domain or realm.

trust relationship. The condition of having established trust.

trusted issuer. A claims provider for which trust has been established with the WS-Trust protocol.

user credentials. A set of credentials. An example is a user name and password.

Web identity. Authenticated identifying characteristics of the sender of an HTTP request. Often, this is an authenticated e-mail address.

Web single sign-on (Web SSO). A process that enables partnering organizations to exchange user authentication and authorization data. By using Web SSO, users in partner organizations can transition between secure Web domains without having to present credentials at each domain boundary.

Windows Communication Foundation (WCF). A component of the Windows operating system that enables Web services.

Windows identity. User information maintained by Active Directory.

Windows Identity Foundation (WIF). A .NET Framework library that enables applications to use claims-based identity and access control.

WS-Federation. The WS-Federation standard defines mechanisms that are used to enable identity, attribute, authentication, and authorization federation across different trust realms. This standard includes an interoperable use of HTTP redirection in order to request security tokens.

WS-Federation Authentication Module (FAM). A component of the Windows Identity Foundation that performs claims processing.

WS-Federation Passive Requestor Profile. WS-Federation Passive Requester Profile describes how the cross-trust realm identity, authentication, and authorization federation mechanisms defined in WS-Federation can be used by passive requesters such as Web browsers to provide identity services. Passive requesters of this profile are limited to the HTTP protocol.

WS-Policy. A Web standard that specifies how Web services may advertise their capabilities and requirements to potential clients.

WS-Security. The WS-Security standard consists of a set of protocols designed to help secure Web service communication using SOAP.

WS-Trust. A standard that takes advantage of WS-Security to provide Web services with methods to build and verify trust relationships.

X.509. A standard format for certificates.

X.509 certificate. A digitally signed statement that includes the issuing authority's public key.v

Index